The Rarest of These is Hope

HAROLD C. WARLICK, JR.

A RESOURCE FOR CHRISTIANS FACING DIFFICULT TIMES

THE RAREST OF THESE IS HOPE

5826/ISBN 0-89536-743-2

For Coulter and Scott,
who challenge and inspire
their mother and father

Table of Contents

Acknowledgements

One spring my wife and I spent ten days in Brussels as the guests of then-NATO Ambassador and lasting family friend, W. Tapley Bennett, Jr. As we traveled through different national and linguistic barriers from our homebase in Brussels, the ambassador carefully cautioned me always to ask for an "allez-retour" ticket. Whatever else might happen, I always felt secure if I could find the "allez-retour" (go and return) printed somewhere on the scrap of paper that served as my passport for travel.

For me, life has always been a "go and return" type of affair. In the professional dimension I have gone into the intoxicating and lively world of Harvard University and returned to the equally lively but more familiar world of the parish ministry. In the geographical dimension I have gone from East to West, South to North, only to return to the state in which I was born. In the ideological dimension I have gone into the concepts and realities of pessimism, secularism, and doubt, only to return to the familiar message of hope which gave my life a new calling several decades ago. Perhaps I am living proof of Paul Tillich's famous sermon on limitations. Life is essentially a tightrope to be walked between living up to your potential and not getting beyond your limitations.

In that tedious, cautious, inch-by-inch stepping onto the tightrope, I have been immeasurably helped by those individuals who have provided me the intellectual security of an "allez-retour" ticket. As I have made my journey through life, a cadre of well-informed friends have kept me honest, called for clarity, and pressed me for sharpness and discernment in my efforts to write and preach about that journey. Perhaps the most important assistance from any quarter for a writer comes from those friends who convince him never to give up the pursuit of written communication. In that respect I am eternally grateful for Robert Blocker of Waco, Texas; William Brown of Jacksonville, Florida; Hal and Paula Wingo of Riverside, Connecticut; and Bob Wynn of Spartanburg, South Carolina. How often I have cherished the "round trip ticket" for life they have unknowingly provided my frame of mind.

I would be grossly remiss if I did not thank the members of Emerywood Baptist Church, High Point, North Carolina, for their constant encouragement and challenge. With a maverick such as I for a pastor, church for them is a realistic and creative struggle. No pastor has more freedom in the pulpit and for that I am grateful. My efforts to discern meaning in

8

life and for life have not had to labor under the heavy cloud of institutional self-interest.

Finally, all love and appreciation to Diane, my wife and most understanding, yet challenging, critic. Without her keen insight, my message would be more impenetrable and cumbersome than it appears to be in its final form.

Introduction

In our day hope seems to be a rare commodity indeed. Whether you are one who worships every Sunday; one who worships now and then; one who avoids the church and what it seems to stand for; or one called to preach to those who worship; you know full well how tough it can be to try to live these days with undiminished hope.

During the past five years I have changed the focus of my preaching. This revision began when my colleague and friend, Dick Devor, asked me to preach in the huge People's Church adjacent to the campus of Michigan State University of East Lansing, Michigan. As I prepared for that assignment, I realized that most of my sermons either focused on "love" in its various manifestations or tried to bring a prophetic word to listeners at ease in Zion. Yet on that occasion I found myself prepared to speak to many individuals in a state which had lost a major portion of its economic stability due to the crisis in the automobile industry. In addition, the university was then in turmoil over proposed faculty reductions, and many of the students I had interviewed about graduate study on previous trips wondered if they would even have a future for themselves and their children in a nuclear age. Whatever was needed from a preacher, it certainly was not a generalized appeal to "love thy neighbor" or a harsh call to involvement in the latest sub-crisis on Main Street. The role of the preacher, if one had a role, was to offer a message of hope beyond the present and to suggest religious meaning for the current demands of living.

As I traveled around the country, fulfilling various speaking engagements, I found that the ethos was the same everywhere. From the bright, energetic black students who came to the services in the Martin Luther King Jr. Chapel on the Morehouse College campus in Atlanta, to the affluent men and women who populated the Greenwich Baptist Church in Greenwich, Connecticut, to the men and women engaged in the urban and financial expansion in Houston, who ate lunch in the Rice Faculty Club and worshiped in the fashionable River Oaks Section, to the thirtieth reunion class of the Harvard Business School which worshiped in historic Old North Church in Boston, and finally to a more permanent place to reside in High Point, North Carolina, furniture capital of America, the people seemed always to ask the same question: "What does your religion have to say about any hope for a meaningful future?"

Indeed, the task of ministry and preaching has changed. No longer do people come in off the rural pathways to hear a minister prod their lethargy or prick their consciences about service or make them aware of personal and societal evil. Those who sit in the pews are experts in these matters. They learn to stare at a television before they learn to read. The six o'clock news can prick millions of consciences and pull a cloud of despair over tens of millions. What people want to know is the meaning, if any, of this nasty business called living. So I have been presumptuous enough to revise my interpretation of the tasks of ministry and preaching. This should not seem out of line, for you and I live in a world which is constantly revising itself. We live with *revised* weather forecasts, *revised* budgets, *revised* economic indicators and a *revised* standard version of the Bible. We recognize that revision is a necessary part of the life experience.

In this respect, I think about the Apostle Paul who wrote so many letters to so many churches. Paul was always revising himself. That's why he wrote so many letters. Each situation was different. He could not drop a note to the Philippians and tell the people to read his previously published letters to Rome. He did not send a message to the people in Thessalonica that they should read his previously published letter to the Philippians. Paul was always bringing God's word into compliance with the needs of a particular place and time.

For this reason, I believe that if Paul were writing a letter to our society for the decade ahead, he probably would refocus his great treatise on love. For the church in Corinth, Paul focused on three virtues: faith, hope, and love. "The greatest of these," he said, "is love."

For the people in our day, I think Paul would focus on hope — if not as the greatest virtue-certainly as the rarest virtue for us in our time. You see, Paul wrote to a society in which the greatest need in Corinth was to define love. The presence of prostitutes in pagan temples had made the word "love" an abomination. Just down the street from the Corinthian Church, prostitutes were blowing trumpets, beating cymbals, and sounding gongs to attract customers. And internally congregational life was a mess. Wealthy members of the church came to the services an hour early in order to take communion and go home in secret so they would not have to sit with the poor people in the regular service.

Love was a rare item in that place. One man, named Paul, stretched his vision above the mediocrity of the times and defined its true nature.

In our times, hope may be the rarest item to find and the one item that needs to be defined. An incredible sense of fatalism hangs over our earth like an ominous cloud in our nuclear age. You and I come together in our churches for worship in a time when society cries out for something to look forward to. We have tried it all; bought it all; been everywhere and seen everything. We now even have the technological capacity to blow it all up.

Several months ago two policemen were walking their beat in the inner city of Detroit, Michigan. They paused in front of a grocery store which was known to house an illegal gambling operation. One officer suggested, "let's go in there and bust it. Let's put the cuffs on them and lead them away." The other officer thought for a moment and smiled. He shook his head as he replied, "No, let's just leave them alone today. We'll bust it tomorrow. People are in there purchasing a number for fifty cents. They have looked into the face of poverty and umemployment. Where else in this town can those people have 'hope' for fifty cents? Let's give them one more day of the cheapest hope in town. We can bust it tomorrow."

You and I are in a strange way a part of that scene, if not physically then certainly attitudinally.

In our own ways we shell out our money and energy trying to fill our needs for *hope* that our future will be meaningful for us. For some among us, it's the hope that the sickness which threatens our bodies or the old age which peeks at us from around the corner will stay away a few more years. For some of us, it's the hope our marriage will get better or, if not, that we can grow stronger as persons than we are at the present time. For others, it's the hope that we can do something to enable our children and our children's children to have a better life or a better community or a better education than we had. For all of us, these and other hopes are what keep us going. The Bible is right, where there is no hope for the future, there is no power to do anything in the present. *Without a vision, the people do indeed perish.*

It is precisely at this point, in our time, that the claims of Jesus of Nazareth should have something to say to us. Frankly, I think they do. As people of hope, you and I must have historical reasons for our hope in this God of ours. It isn't enough to know that we can stand alone in the face of death with God at our side and be turned to dust with the promise of individual salvation. *That isn't enough!* We must have hope for the larger units of which we are a part — hope for our families; hope for our nations; hope for our churches; hope for our communities. If salvation only covers my life and leaves out my family, my community, and my world, it is not a very comprehensive guarantee, is it? *The people perish without a vision for the people,* just as the individual perishes without a vision for the individual.

The procession of Christ and his disciples who slowly entered into

Jerusalem so long ago, was a vision of hope for the *people*. The kingdom of God was at hand, not just a smattering of individual salvation policies. It finally came. *Or did it?* Jesus spoke of a new heaven and a new earth; a new covenant and a new kingdom.

But it did not appear that anything had come. Those on the top of the social ladder stayed on top even after Jesus' death; those on the bottom stayed on the bottom. The scars of divisiveness, bitterness, and war still scarred the political landscape in the Middle East and remain even as I write. But the kingdom of God *had come*. The end times were being lived out, even if the world was not quite there yet.

Theologians call Jesus' approach "eschatological" which means looking toward the end times. Jesus confronted the world not with the claims of the present but with the end times. That's the hope of the world — being able to live *now* in the end times, being a part in the *present* of that which is to come.

That is the only hope we can cling to in any age. You and I must live our life together in anticipation of that which the world does not yet have. Our common life must be a foretaste of the end times, not just the present. We must live our life together as if the churches in this world have more unity than they actually have; we must live *our* life together as if the world has more love than it actually has; we must live *our* life together as if our society has more justice than it actually has. This is not to say that we are any better than other groups. We may not be as good as many. But *I believe that it is profoundly important for some people to live their lives in anticipation of that which the world does not yet have.*

But how do we do that in a way which brings hope to ourselves and others? I think it's best defined in a parable told by Abraham Heschel.[1] The parable is about a kingdom in which the grain crop was poisoned. Everyone who ate the grain went crazy. But because there were few other food supplies, the people were faced with a horrible choice: They could eat the grain and go insane or not eat the grain and starve to death. Surveying the situation, the king said, "Very well then, let us eat the grain, for we cannot starve. But let us at the same time feed a few people on a different diet so we will at least have some people who will know that we are insane and can tell us so."

Humanity has eaten poisoned food. It did in the time of Jesus and it still does today. It eats the food of monetary greed, military hardware, racial prejudice, idolatry, and religious divisiveness. The message of Christ is that you and I must be those who are pulled aside to eat a different diet. *We feed on the things of the end times:* prayer, love and justice, intellectual integrity, and the vision of peace when the lion and lamb lie down together and every hill is made low.

The Christian task is to find contemporary ways of communicating to a hopeless world that hope abounds in the midst of its craziness.

That is precisely the task accepted in the following pages. As we together examine images of hope, expressions of hopeful service, reinterpretations of lifestyles, and dimensions of hope in a troubled world, it is the author's desire to paint for the reader some pictures of a needed vision for our time.

Part One

The Images of Hope

1

' A God With Skin On

One of my favorite authors is the great Robert Louis Stevenson. I especially delight in his frightening fable of Dr. Jekyll and Mr. Hyde. Dr. Jekyll is a kind, respectable physician. But he discovers a drug which enables him to change his appearance and his personality. He can, at will, lose his respectability and become the depraved Mr. Hyde. Soon he begins to find increasing delight in pursuing forbidden pleasures. He tries to refrain from taking the drug which turns him into Mr. Hyde, but his lower nature and lower values torment him until once again he swallows the transforming drug. Dr. Jekyll's words are prophetic: "My devil had long been caged. He came out roaring. The spirit of hell awoke within me and raged."

His lower self, so long chained down, begins to get the upper hand in his personality. Dr. Jekyll learns the terrible truth: A person is not just one person, but can truly be two people. There are both good and bad elements fighting for control over human personalities.

In this respect, we can understand the battle for values which took place between Moses and the children of Israel at Sinai. As long as the people could have Moses with them, they tended to be fine. Moses was an image of God. But when Moses left the people and went up the mountain, the people became anxious. They went to Aaron and asked him to make an image they could see. They formed a golden calf and began to traffic in their lower nature. You see, in the land of Egypt, the children of Israel had been exposed to the worst images of human depravity and such exposure is not easily shaken from one's memory. In Dr. Jekyll's words: "Their devil had been caged and he came out roaring."

The children of Israel and Dr. Jekyll learned what most of us know: experiences in life rub off on us, even if we don't want them to. Even when we look at our lower nature only by accident, it's a battle to keep it repressed. The late, great statesman, Dag Hammarskjold put it like this: "You cannot play with the animal in you without becoming wholly animal, play with falsehood without forfeiting your right to truth, play with cruelty without losing your sensitivity of mind."

You and I do not play with our lower natures to any conscious degree. But we are exposed to *appeals* to those natures perhaps more than any other generation in history. We have to fight hard to live up to our images of hope in God. Most of the advertising in our world appeals more to our animal than spiritual nature. Our newspapers and televisions report more images of despair than images of hope. We know far more about the evil in the world than the world's good. We have come through a sexual revolution. We are exposed to both holiness and defilement. Whether we call it the lower nature, Satan, or sin, matters little. The fact remains that you and I have to fight the battle that every saint has had to fight since the beginning of time — *The battle for control of our own lives.* We have to constantly repress and conquer our worst selves. It is our Christian effort to be our best selves and not our worst selves in the places where life has called us to live. P. T. Forsyth is correct: "The resurrection of Christ is a victory in a battle, not an answer to a riddle."

Consequently, our Bible is a collection of images of hope not merely answers to riddles about life and death. You and I live with images. We think in pictures. We model the people that we see. We do not fight our battles for personhood in the arena of detached questions and answers. We have to have something we can touch and feel and see. If it isn't a Moses or a tablet of stones, it will be a golden calf.

A small child was in her bed asleep one night when a huge thunderstorm rolled across the plains where she and her family lived. When the lightning began to flash and the thunder sounded, it frightened her. As children do in such occasions, she sat up in bed and screamed for her mommy and daddy. The parents came rushing into the room and the father calmly put his arms around her and said, "Go back to sleep. Don't worry, God is here. God will take care of you."

So the little girl went back to sleep. But a few minutes later the thunder and lightning came again. Once again the little girl sat up in bed and screamed. When the parents had entered the room, she anticipated their response. So she quickly stated, "Mommy, Daddy, I know God is here and God will take care of me, but *I need somebody in this room with skin on them.*"

We, as humans, need to have both abstract ideas about God and tangible images of God that we can reach out and touch and identify with. The golden calf was a low image of the lower self, but you could touch it and identify with it. The word of God on stone tablets was a higher image of a higher hope that those people could also touch. A washed-out vagabond, a prodigal son who has squandered his father's money and is eating slop from an animal feeder is a low image we can identify with. But a banquet table prepared by a loving father is a higher image of a better self that we can also hope for.

The early church understaood the importance of worthy images to hope in. Paul wrote to the Romans that God's will for us is that we be "conformed to the *image* of his son, Jesus Christ."

We must uphold the image of Christ because our children and children's children are shaped by images. The awesome facts of hereditary images are cited throughout the Bible. In scripture, the claim is made that the images of the parents are visited upon the children to the third and fourth generations. And its true. Some genealogists[2] have laboriously uncovered instructive statistics. Look backwards for a moment at the impact of two 18th century families.

Jonathan Edwards, was a Congregational minister in Massachusetts. He had a lot of personal shortcomings. But he upheld the image of Jesus Christ as he knew that image in his day and time. Edwards was born in 1703. Within two hundred years, there were 1,400 identified descendants of Jonathan Edwards. Thirteen were college presidents; sixty-one were physicians; sixty-five were college professors; over one hundred were ministers; over one hundred were lawyers and over two hundred were in social service careers.

In 1720 the progenitor of the famous Jukes family was born. He never upheld any image of any church or faith much less of Jesus Christ. He was simply a petty criminal. His descendants over the two hundred years since his birth can also be readily identified.

Over 1,200 of those descendants spent most of their lives in penal institutions. Fifty became notorious prostitutes and seven were murderers.

Is this coincidence? Is the analysis too simplistic? Or do we really live by images and find that indeed the images of the parents are visited upon the children to the third and fourth generations?

Most of us have principles that we espouse. But when it comes to waging the battle in our lives between good and evil, I think most of us go with what we've experienced. *Herein lies the real strength of a church. Participation in fellowship and worship causes us, even if unconsciously, to traffic among the highest images available to us.* Being conformed to the images of the empty tomb, the communion table, the cross, and the Bible, helps us marshal resources in the battle we all have to wage to be our most hopeful self. Whether it be in our morals, our prejudices, our use of finances, our treatment of employees, or in a hundred and one other issues, you and I bring to our existence no more or no less than what we have experienced.

Merely attending church is no guarantee of a quality life. Perhaps there are legitimate complaints about the brick and mortar costs of church buildings and even the flaws in the personalities present in churches. But we live by images. And we must have a God with skin on him. We must have images, even of brick and mortar, that we can let filter into our consciousness.

Perhaps the easiest image to develop is that of a circle. Imagine yourself as a circle, divided in half, half of which is composed of hope and half of which is composed of despair. The hopeful side contains such images as your mother's furniture, the devotions and poetry you have read, the scriptures, the people who have been kind to you in life, the dependence of your children on you, the quality sermons you have heard, and moments of stray fun. All those positive images you possess belong on that side.

The other half of the circle contains the depressing images of life — The threat of nuclear war, the mean-spirited and painful people you have met, the anxieties that shadow us and the glass bottom boat ride through the sewer that we call human evil.

There are certain people and images in life which can cause that axis to be tilted maybe even just a fraction of a percent, from the despair toward hope. By the presence in our lives of worthy images we can reclaim a wedge of our hopeful self.

This is the life-long benefit of participation in a hopeful community and belief in a loving God. The hopeful images creep over. Whether we call it the leaven in the loaf, the seed which falls on good ground, the pearl of great value, or whatever, the axis is shifted and the hopeful images creep over. Especially is this true relative to our opinion of God. Within our consciousness our hope in a loving God wages a war with our fear of a terrible God.

No image of hope can be complete without a vision of a loving God, a God who suffers lovingly for us and with us, one who will embrace us when we're terrified — a God with skin on!

2

God Is Not the Bogey Man

When I was a child one of my favorite stories was that of the marvelous puppet-turned-boy, Pinocchio. You will remember Pinocchio had a unique characteristic: every time he told a lie his nose would grow longer. Many an evening I went to bed in great anxiety, certain that when I awoke the next morning my nose would have grown longer because of the day's falsehoods. It was always a relief to awake in the morning and find the same short nose anchored to the face I saw in the bathroom mirror. As I grew older, of course, I learned that people's noses do not serve as lie detectors.

But to a degree, we humans do possess bodily indicators of guilt. When someone asks us an incriminating question our breathing and heart rate change. This fact of anatomy leads us to a booming business in lie-detector machines. Millions of job applicants are now subjected to polygraph tests. And insurance companies use such tests for those who apply for compensation for injuries.

Strangely enough, many persons in our world view God as a cosmic lie-detector machine. God is "the big eye in the sky," seeing everything we do and recording it. God's big ears are everywhere, absorbing our quietest whispers. Whenever failure takes place, we experience great fear because "the big man upstairs knows it all."

At times the minister of a church is seen as one whose main job is to preach a fear of punishment from this all-knowing God. The more he can terrify his audience of hell, the better he considers his message. *Christianity is thus seen as living in fear of dreadful vengeance by God for sin.*

As a Baptist, I grew up on a steady diet of this kind of preaching. The sage Soren Kierkegaard summarized the feeling. After listening to a particular sermon on Sunday, Kierkegaard remarked, "I feel as if I have been trampled to death by a flock of geese."

It is quite a feeling always to fear that somehow somewhere God is going to take great pleasure in getting even with us. *Some misguided people are actually frightened of God.* They believe God to be a strict, unyielding, and overpowering person who wants us to relate to him with feelings of fear. In such cases, punishment is welcomed because it relieves them of their guilt. It is very hard for life to be hopeful in such circumstances.

The most graphic illustration I know of this principle is a man I shall call Larry. I met Larry in a class I taught for alcoholics. Larry was congenial and outgoing, with a fine sense of humor. His ability to articulate his deepest personal feelings thrust him into the position of class spokesman.

Yet underneath the exterior lay a complexity of personal problems. Larry had tried to commit suicide seven times.

Larry did well for months at a time. He held down a high-salaried job and was one of his company's better employees when he was sober. Then once a month or more it would happen. The alcohol abuse counselor and I would receive a call. Larry would be stone drunk and screaming. He would imagine spiders and snakes crawling all over his body. We would rush to his home and help him brush off the imaginary "spiders and snakes." Occasionally he became so terrified that we had to transport him to the hospital where the doctors and nurses used brushes and brooms to convince him that all the bugs and reptiles had been killed.

At the root of Larry's problem is a deep-seated fear of God. Larry had some domestic problems that grew into an intense conflict. Before he knew it, alcohol had become his escape. One night Larry attended a revival his minister was conducting. The minister preached one of those "trampled-to-death-by-geese" sermons, and Larry responded. Larry honestly wanted to change his behavioral patterns. So when the service was over the minister gave Larry a Bible, and told him that if he read it and prayed to Jesus his troubles with alcohol would be over.

Now, one does not let such a find as Larry pass out of reach. So the minster coerced Larry into standing before the church to give his testimony. It was a spellbinding story. Soon Larry was persuaded that he had a story he should "tell to the nations". So Larry sold his possessions and moved to Kentucky to attend the Bible institute. All went well — for two weeks. Then the conflicts, still unresolved, began to re-emerge and Larry hit the bottle again. But this time a guilt like he had never felt before set in. He was plagued with fears of punishment by God. Soon a pattern was established that persists to this day. The imaginary spiders and snakes are, for Larry, signs of God's punishment. He feels better after they have crawled over him. Once the punishment period ends, he sells everything again and heads back to Kentucky to the Bible institute. There he lives in terror that he'll slip in his behavior.

Three psychiatrists, a counselor, and I labored for three years to unseat Larry's image of God as a wrathful vindicator. We never made a dent.

While Larry's case is extreme, the people who are troubled by confused concepts of God are many. Most of us grew up with the impression God's love is something to be earned. God loves only those who love God. From childhood days God is presented as one who punishes. Perhaps a teacher reminded us that hell is a resting place for those who tell fibs; or a preacher screamed at us the wages of sin is death. Sin, of course meant dancing, gambling, playing cards, going to the movies, and other such major distractions.

Many of us learned to pray in fear. We learned to worship in fear.

I once asked a group of children to draw a picture of God. One child drew a lightning bolt striking a cluster of stick people. "What's that?" I asked. "God killing all the bad people," was the reply.

Now the teachers, ministers, and parents behind such explanations are often well-meaning. We should be God fearing. *On the other hand, they perhaps also find the fear of God very convenient as a tool for controlling behavior.* Some ministers also find fear of God to be a very convenient tool for church growth. But such negative imagery becomes counterproductive in the lives of persons seeking to find hope in the midst of an entire world of negatives. Professor of Management, Peter Drucker, is correct: "A success which has outlived its usefulness may, in the long run, be worse than a failure."[3]

Jesus Christ did not preach a tyrannical God of wrath and superstition. This is all the more amazing when we consider that he lived and preached in a place and time when mystery religions were making such claims.

Jesus met head-on the issue of reprisals from God. Recorded in the ninth chapter of John's Gospel is Jesus' encounter with a blind beggar. Apparently some people in the community had been pointing to this poor man as evidence of what happens when a person sins against God. Certainly if this man had not sinned, then his parents must have. People could understand misfortune in these terms. Jesus refuted the notion that God works with such vengeance. "Who sinned, this man or his parents," asked the disciples. Jesus answered: "It was *not* that this man sinned or his parents."

Jesus' main concern was that humankind understand God as a God of love and not a God of hatred. You see, Jewish legalism had produced a frightening picture of God. In the Old Testament we see a God who is accompanied by loud and awesome trumpet blasts. We encounter a God whose messages were so terrible that people begged him to stop speaking. Moses, frightened at the sight of God on the mountain, shook with a terrible fear.

Along with this image of God came a frightening vision of a place called hell. In the Old Testament the worst place people could image was the garbage dump outside Jerusalem, the Valley of Hinnom. Fire burned there all the time. All unclaimed corpses and useless garbage were placed there. The book of Revelation and the book of Hebrews, easily the most Jewish material in the New Testament, captured that image for hell. "It's a lake of fire," said these Jews, "where individuals die a second death."

Jesus rejected the Hebrew idea of eternal physical pain inflicted by a vindictive God as punishment for human failure. He spoke of outer darkness, where people are isolated from each other and from God. There exists weeping and wailing and gnashing of teeth because people are frustrated due to their unfulfillment. They are cut of from that which gives their lives meaning.

You see, hell is our refusal to enter into relationship with God. We have blamed hell on the wrong party. We have depicted hell as a place which God created out of God's displeasure and to which God sends rebellious persons. Hell is a state God permits, not a place God has created.

But God takes our freedom seriously. God does not force us against our wills. God does not want us to be ultimately separated but God allows it if we so choose. Hell is against what God wants. God does not like it. But God *permits* it. God lets us choose separation if we wish. But God hopes we will not choose it.

In Luke's gospel the Pharisees and Scribes are murmuring against Jesus because he is eating with sinners. They think Jesus doesn't come down hard enough on sin; that he "is not preaching hell." So Jesus tells a parable which describes what eternal judgment is like. The parable of the prodigal son is Jesus' commentary on the issue of heaven and hell. A younger son comes to his senses and returns home to his father. The overjoyed father decides to throw a huge party. He makes forgiveness a joyful experience.

Suddenly the oldest son comes in and is appalled at what he sees. He believes that his father is too soft-hearted. The father's delight turns his stomach. The party atmosphere repulses him. He turns away. He will not come to the party. The father invites the older son to join the festivities, thinking he may catch the spirit. But this son is so set against the father's joy that he will not enter. *He chooses to stay outside in the darkness.* The father does not coerce him. He does not force him to come to the party and pretend he's having a good time. He allows the oldest son to remain in the darkness, cut off from the party. Love does not force anyone against their will. Love that allows freedom of choice allows the freedom to forever remain cut off from God's fellowship. That's the response Jesus gave when asked about heaven and hell.

The problem of hell or eternal separation from God is our problem, not God's problem. God takes our freedom seriously.

Consequently *God does not frighten me.* God is no cosmic bogey-man. Instead, God has shown a tremendous affection for this planet. God wants all of us to come to the banquet that is prepared for us. God wants us to feast together eternally. God so loved us that he sent his only son to draw us to him. And when that did not work, that son laid down his life to draw us to the banquet of heaven. God is a god of loving kindness.

No, God does not frighten me. The only thing we have to fear is that we will not be satisfied with the gift of love and the personal relationship which God, as father, offers us.

Such an image of God as a loving parent provides hope for us as we respond to the images of life. But this hope does not come easily. Transforming a life from despair into hope takes a long time. And it has consequences far into our future. Abundant instead of fearful living involves no small exodus. Taking the journey from despondency into the hope of God may entail the longest distance between two points.

3

The Long Way Around:
You Can Get There From Here

Exodus is more than a word for an ancient journey. It is a permanent condition of every Christian this side of heaven. We are always being liberated from our slavery to certain ideas, stations in life and people. Likewise we often find ourselves slipping from the freedom of controlling our life to the *slavery* of certain attitudes and preconceptions which only make us think and feel that we are free. Yes, we are always moving from bondage to freedom to bondage to freedom.

Life is full of people trying to make an exodus from what they consider to be a particular problem. One of the most amusing issues, of course, is our effort to deal with aging. All of us are aging and we are, in effect, in bondage to the aging process. Sonny Throckmorton has authored a song about a person who tries to get away from aging and find the promised land. The song is about a person called "Middle Age Crazy". Middle Age Crazy has just reached his 40th birthday. He trades his Oldsmobile for a new Porsche car and his gray business suit for jeans and high heeled boots with an embroidered star. Middle Age Crazy is bald on top and he's quite a sight to see. He had a wife he had loved for a long time but the thrill is gone. He and his wife spent a while building up a business but the long, uphill climb is now over and profits are high. So he dumps his wife. Forty years old going on twenty, he has a sweet young thing beside him that just melts in his hand. And she understands that he's Middle Age Crazy, trying to prove that he's still a man.

The story of Middle Age Crazy is a tragedy. An individual tries to become liberated from despair. Breaking free from the bondage of his past he thinks he will find hope but, instead falls victim to another form of bondage. His cure becomes worse than his disease.

All of us find ourselves in need of exodus. There are times when self-acceptance is hard to come by and we are tempted to try to leave that situation, life-style or perspective. Sometimes, however, what we could *go to* is worse than what we *got out of*. A particular experience in my own life leaps into my consciousness. Shortly after arriving in Boston to begin my seminary career I was assigned a job as Assistant Minister in Park Avenue Congregational Church. Such an assignment pleased me. What more could you ask for than to work at the corner of Park Avenue and Paul Revere Road? All went well in the preliminary arrangements which lasted through the fall. New assignments were comfortably handled. Then came time for the church Christmas party. It was held in the parlor of a beautiful home and I ventured there with great anticipation. One of the church members was a professor in the New England Conservatory of Music. The entertainment for that evening consisted of that woman playing "Jingle Bells" on the piano in the style of various composers, with the church members trying to guess which composer would have written the song that way. For over an hour I sat there surrounded by people shouting out "Wagner, Beethoven, Bach, Mozart, Schubert," etc., while I just sat there and stared with my mouth open.

I returned to the dormitory that night totally deflated. It just would not work. If that was "class," I certainly did not have it. So I sat down and wrote out my letter of resignation. I reasoned that I would carry it to the chairman of the personnel committee. He was a "class" person and would understand when I told him I couldn't make the jump from South Carolina to genuine musical sophistication.

I went up to the floor of the building where this person worked. As I sat in the office, letter of resignation in hand, his secretary came out to tell me that Mr. Hanson was very busy. He hadn't slept much the night before and his phone had been ringing all morning. Finally after what seemed to be an agonizing wait, Mr. Hanson, bleary-eyed and with his tie unloosened came into the lobby. "Come in, Mr. Warlick," he said. "Pardon my appearance but a few church members rang my phone off the hook last night griping about the god-awful Christmas party. What a disaster.

Nobody knew what was happening. We kept throwing out every composer's name we knew, hoping that every now and then we'd hit the target and get the blasted evening over with. Wasn't it awful?"

"Yes, it was," I responded. "Well?" he asked. "Well what?" I countered. "What did you come to see me about?" he quizzed. "Nothing. Nothing at all," I answered. "I was just passing by."

I began that day by taking little baby steps into getting to know some of the dearest friends I would ever have. I shudder when I think that I almost made a quiet exodus from a minor discomfort into an even worse form of slavery, that of forever feeling rejected. The slavery of self-rejection is a great slavery. Through a minor misunderstanding I almost strereotyped an entire people.

All of us have those moments when we have to deal with the exodus desire. Most of us in our athletic endeavors, our student life, our business life, our family life or our pleasure life face a time when we might be tempted to think we'd be better off quitting. The point is this: *just escaping a perceived bondage does not always lead to freedom.* Whether it be the "Middle Age Crazy" my "Jingle Bells" experience, or a host of *your* situations in life, *how we effect freedom is more important than freedom itself.*

Jesus the Christ told a disturbing parable about an empty house. A house is in bondage to a problem, an unclean spirit. We are told the owner kicks the spirit out. *The owner has won.* But *a house cannot remain* empty. Since the owner does not replace the evil with good, the evil returns and seven other devils accompany it. Thus, the house is liberated from the bondage to one spirit in order to be free to be in bondage to eight spirits. Jesus is articulating a situation that happens when we seek freedom without replacing it *with responsibility.* Therefore, how one is freed and for what end are the crucial issues in liberation. Because none of us remains empty.

One of the disturbing aspects of the hopelessness in today's world is its contribution to fly-by-night religious hucksters. Many people are fleeing their perceived states of doubt and negativism about life straight into the arms of television evangelists and superficial hucksters who claim to put band-aids on their wounded hearts and can at the same time liberate their cash while promising genuine hope for the future. Such quick claim, fix-it religious entrepreneurs leave their victims in worse shape than before. Theirs is not a quiet journey from despair into a lasting hope.

One of the amazing facts of scripture is that Satan is very seldom pictured as ugly and hideous. In fact most of the time, from the temptations of Jesus to the cross, *evil is presented as the most handsome and attractive way out of a mess.*

Perhaps this helps us understand the call of Israel out of Egypt and our call to be the people of God in our day. We are told that the Israelites made a courageous exodus from Egypt. God overcomes Pharaoh and they are delivered. But, amazingly enough, God does not lead the Israelites to the Promised Land by the shortest route. They do not go along the northern edge of the Suez and then along the cost of Gaza. That journey would have taken two weeks at the most. *Two weeks!* Here are people who had been in Egyptian slavery *215 years.* They finally are freed and head for the land of promise only two weeks away. But God doesn't lead that direct way. The way God leads them takes *40 years! Why?*

Scripture says that the near path led through the land of the Philistines. The people might see war and run from it. But read the scripture again. *The people might see war and win and like it.* The Bible tells us that the children of Israel "went out of the land of Egypt equipped for battle." They were ready to fight. They had been caged up and downtrodden. They were now strong. They had their history with them and they even carried the bones of their original charter member, Joseph. They had been mighty enough to conquer Pharaoh. They were armed physically with military hardware, and armed psychologically with the bones of Joseph. They were liberated. They were like Middle Age Crazy. They had traded in their slave clothing for military armor and they had the bones of Joseph by their side. They were the children of Israel trying to prove they could be a man — trying to prove they could be mighty like the rest of the young nations at that time.

But freedom from bondage was not God's total intent with these people. *They were not freed because God needed successful, arrogant smart alecks.* The people were freed in order to bear witness to a God of love and service. Had the Israelites traveled the two-week path, win or lose, they would have escaped the bondage of one evil, Egypt, only to acquire bondage to even worse evils like arrogance, triumphalism, vanity, and greed. Yes, how a person is freed and for what end is crucial. *Those people were freed to witness effectively to a God who is morally and spiritually good and thereby change the attitudes of the world.*

That, too, is the meaning of our liberation in Jesus Christ from the bondage of despair. We embrace hope in God to bear witness to moral and spiritual goodness. Our marching orders always demand that we take the long way around. The exodus experience provides an interesting commentary on great accomplishments. Great achievements succeed only in steps of time and only in harmony with responsibility. Look at what happened to those people in over 40 years. The impulse to hurt was transformed into the desire to bless. Savageness was channelled into commitment. The people began to move from the way of the tiger to the way of the lamb. Even the "eye for an eye and a tooth for a tooth" which seems so savage to us was an improvement for those people. Prior to that, if a tribe member put out the eye of a member of your tribe, you got your tribe and wiped out his tribe; men, women, and children slaughtered all for the sake of an eye. Yes, the way of the lamb had begun.

It takes strength to bear witness to a God of love.

To be certain, Israel did not totally live and move in the way of the lamb. Hostility, antagonism, and deceit fill many pages of the Old Testament. But her exodus was a beginning of the little baby steps of time. Out of her long history came a revelation that climaxed when Christ culminated the "Way of the Lamb."

You and I are always traveling from despair toward hope and back again. That movement seems to be a permanent condition of the human race. Always there are new freedoms to be obtained, new challenges to be met, and new life styles beckoning us. But how we succeed in that movement and to what ends are crucial. We are called to take the long way around. That's harder. It means we must go the first hopeful mile before we can go the second. But the difficult way of service is the only way to give lasting hope for that is the only way to bear witness to a God of loving-kindness.

4

Hope's First Mile

One of the realities in today's world is the fact that so many of us have become stereotyped or type-cast by our professions. This is as true for people in the world of business as it is for people from the world of ministry. I was reminded of this salient fact one day when the Dean of Harvard Divinity School tapped me on the shoulder and informed me that I was to go over to Old North Church in Boston and preach a good "business executive sermon," to the members of a Harvard Business School class celebrating their 30th reunion. I'm not certain what a good business executive sermon is! In my experiences in ministering to executives in the churches I have pastored, I have found that those executives have defined and articulated their own religious perceptions pretty much the same as have other members of the human race. They certainly do not differentiate themselves apart from human experience.

A particular problem in relating to segments of the business community lies, I believe, in the fact that religion has too often been presented in a generalized way. We seem to postpone our message to the second mile of existence without focusing on the vitality of Christ's message of hope for the "near at hand." My thinking on this matter was informed by an encounter I had with a New York banker. The encounter took place aboard a commercial airline flight I took from Boston through Atlanta. I found myself in a plane circling Atlanta awaiting clearance to land at the very time my connecting flight for my final destination departed below us. I joined several other passengers in audibly lamenting our situation. A passenger sitting across the aisle from me heard me mention my destination. He introduced himself to me and informed me that his final destination was only forty miles from mine, so he shared the same predicament with me. When

I introduced myself to him as a teacher, administrator, and preacher on my way to deliver a sermon, his face lit up and he remarked that he had graduated from Harvard Business School and was the president of a large bank in New York City. We immediately decided to rent a car and drive to our respective engagements while exchanging pleasant talk about religion and business.

Now, I assumed that all New York executives, especially bank presidents, carry major credit cards when they travel. Unfortunately my newly-found traveling companion assumed the same about me. But, alas, both of us had left our major credit cards at home.

You cannot rent a car without a major credit card, or so state the rules! With our luggage in tow we moved despondently through the desks of a half-dozen car rental agencies, encountering rudeness, crassness, condescending remarks, and dead-pan faces. Finally, we decided to wait an hour until the shifts changed and then rush through the counters hoping to catch some new arrival off-guard. It worked. We found a compassionate person who after much persuasion made a call and gave us the keys to a rental car.

As we traveled toward our engagements, my companion inquired of me, "So you're going to preach. What are you going to preach on?" I proudly answered, "Going the *second* mile."

"My God," he exclaimed. "Going the *second* mile. After all we've been through today, you're going to preach on going the *second* mile. That's the problem in our world. You preachers are preaching on going the second mile but nobody in today's world is going the *first* mile. You should preach on going the *first* mile. That's where we need help. That's where we need to find hope."

I have thought about that conversation many times as I have attempted to offer hope to many individuals and have concluded my business friend is quite correct. You see, in the times of Jesus of Nazereth, the Mediterranean area operated under strict hospitality laws. Most people traveled on foot and routine trips took several days. There were no inns or motels like we have today. Consequently the law required the head of the household in each town to journey to the center of town at a certain hour each day, encounter any strangers gathered there and escort a strange family to their home. You had to pull yourself away from your business, feed the stranger's family, and bed and water the animals for a maximum of three days. That was the law and heavy fines were levied on those who did not obey it. Obviously, when you or your family traveled to a strange city, you were at the mercy of the extent to which that city enforced those same laws. Likewise the Roman government required a person to help a soldier carry a burden exactly *one mile*. Again, you were subject to a heavy fine if you disobeyed.

Jesus of Nazareth expected his disciples to be kinder than the laws required. So he commanded them to go beyond the obligation.

Now, you and I do not even operate under a legal mandate to show hospitality. For you and me, the foretaste of the Kingdom of God is bringing the gifts of God into the *first* mile of our existence, into our *jobs* and into our *homes*.

If the world is to find a hopeful existence, it will not find it in platitudes uttered about the second mile of life. The way parents, spouses, executives, merchants, homemakers, grandparents and retirees, conduct their daily lives will bear more witness to the hope of the world than anything else that is done or not done in the name of God.

Jesus was quite clear on this score. When questioned as to our greatest responsibility, his answer was direct: love God with all your heart, mind, and soul and your neighbor as yourself. He demanded a compassionate heart and an open mind, but he focused them on right relations with those around us, in the first mile of life. Likewise Paul and John spoke of the two gifts of the Holy Spirit as being a *compassionate heart* and an *open mind*.

As he so often did, Jesus cemented this perspective with a poignant parable. His parable was about a businessman who brought a compassionate heart and an open mind to his job. The parables of Jesus in general are not very detailed. When we do find one laid out in intricate detail, we can be fairly certain that each of those details is crucial for understanding what Jesus was trying to say. Such a detailed parable is the one you and I know as the parable of the Good Samaritan. But amazingly enough, the real hero in that story received little attention through the years. The true (real) hero is the *innkeeper*. Jesus could have made his point by simply stating that a Levite and a priest passed by a wounded traveler and a Samaritan stopped to help. But notice all the little details about the innkeeper. The exact amount of money paid him and the words of the Good Samaritan to him are meticulously recorded. And with good purpose. You see, Jesus' audience consisted mainly of people from the business and domestic communities. They must have been shocked to hear of a fellow businessman, an innkeeper, who took money from and even extended credit to a Samaritan.

The Good Samaritan simply shelled out some money, established a line of credit and kept on going. *He made an effective referral.* Without the Jewish innkeeper's compassion and tolerance, he would have been helpless. The Good Samaritan's ideology would have remained just that — a good idea that couldn't be implemented!

Jesus hits us between the eyes in this parable. It's probably easier to write a check, make a contribution of money to a worthy cause, or offer some salient words of advice than it is to risk personal involvement. The Good Samaritan sacrificed a few hours out of his trip and some cash out of his pocket. But the innkeeper probably faced losing his reputation. His business surely would have been hurt, maybe even boycotted. He put his career on the line as a witness of God's love and tolerance. *That's harder to do.*

If we miss any part of Jesus' commandment to bring compassion and tolerance into the first mile of life, our jobs and our homes, *we have missed it all.* Tolerance and open-mindedness are in themselves not the key to life. There is not much "hope" in viewing life as merely an event that happens in which one is to always respond only on the level of an open mind. An open mind without a compassionate heart is only a pious scream in the air. Only a small portion of the misery, loneliness, and suffering in this world will be alleviated by those who benevolently dole out their money and advice. Little hope for the goodness of human interaction is felt by recipients of checks given by removed, behind-the-scenes benefactors, although those are necessary. History has paraded that reality across our horizons in numerous examples. Perhaps the most glaring example was that of Jean-Jacques Rousseau.[4]

Few individuals in history have articulated more wisdom about human rights than Rousseau. Yet this same creature lived with a common law wife who bore him five children. After the birth of each child, he sneaked through the dark and left each child on the steps of a hospital. He did not want the responsibility of raising children. Then, when his mistress could bear no more children and the hospital had raised his own, he legally married her. He reasoned that his huge ambitions for society left him little time or energy to spend raising children or contributing even to his neighbors. He was so hell-bent on being *productive* that the reproductive side of life — raising children and concentrating on religious implementations — took a back seat. Needless to say, many people in that society did not care if Rousseau's great mind was productive or not. For them, all his success was cancelled out by his cold heart toward those around him. Those who walk only with an open mind, walk not very far, and offer little in the way of real hope to their contemporaries.

Likewise a compassionate heart without an open mind is only intolerant affection, a condition Jesus referred to as *blindness.* The Apostle Peter, early in his career evidenced a compassionate heart and a small mind. You'll remember at one point he went from gate keeper to the kingdom of heaven to Satan in Jesus' mind in only three short verses.

Scholars have recently translated some gospels which are older than Matthew, Mark, Luke, and John. Those gnostic gospels are important because they shed light on the activities of the early church.[5] One such gospel is the *Gospel of Faith Wisdom* which chronicles some of the events in the lives of Peter and Mary Magdalene. Apparently Peter constantly complained to Jesus that Mary dominated conversations with Jesus. She could speak freely to Jesus but not to Peter, because, in her words, "Peter makes me hesitate; I am afraid of him, because he hates the female race." Jesus replied, "Peter's wrong."

Yes, a compassionate heart can be compassionate at a very low ethical level, when it is not accompanied by tolerance.

This is what makes Pentecost such an exciting event for me. The gift of the Holy Spirit came upon the disciples and Peter preached in a language everyone could understand. The gift of an open mind came to Peter and he began to be sensitive to other peoples' understandings and value them. He opened himself to the possibility that his own language was a myopic one.

The marvelous challenge — to bring together compassion and tolerance in the *first mile of life* — holds the key to enduring hope in our time. Without a witness to good in the first mile of existence, all the planning and positioning of religious values would be like the Good Samaritan without an innkeeper: Good ideas and correct ideals but no power to get things done.

The facts speak loudly. A study was done to determine why Protestants in America participate in particular churches. Five reasons were pinpointed: good Sunday School programs, good recreation programs, quality preaching, prior personal relationships with members at work in the community, and the personality of the pastor. Guess which ranked last in the reasons given for religious participation? The personality of the pastor! The item ranking next to the last was the quality of the preaching. The item which ranked first, which 53 percent of the people gave as the reason they participate in religious life was prior personal relationships with other members in their jobs and in their community.

What religious professionals do in the second mile of life is not nearly as hopeful as what non-professionsals do in the *first* mile of life. If we are to regain hope in ourselves, our God, and our future we must discover the service aspect of our religious traditions in a time when mass-communication capabilities have upped the value on talking and reading about religious experience.

5

Hope Talks Less, Does More

Normally items in the newspaper do not have a chilling impact on me. I guess we have all become so hardened that even the most tragic occurrences hardly prick our emotions. But an article in the paper summoned a host of feelings and memories within me. The article was about a member of the infamous Charles Manson family who had murdered actress Sharon Tate and many others some years ago. This particular person was up for parole and the matter was quite newsworthy.

The material took me back to a day many years ago when a friend of mine asked me to come over to his office. This particular friend owns a religious publishing company. Like most such companies, many of its publications are simply the written accounts of verbal Christian testimonies by famous people. If you are a successful athlete or coach or a reigning or not-too-far-past Miss America or a singing cowboy or cowgirl or a movie star, *your* words about Jesus can get into print. There's a ready market for such important "words" about Jesus from the stars. But in recent years a new market has exploded on the scene. If you are a criminal, with a sordid past, and can tell your story of how you found Jesus in prison, the publishing world will beat a path to your door or cell. In fact, the larger and more brutal the crime, the greater the potential for your material to be gobbled up by the Christian public.

My publisher friend had just that day returned from a prison where he had met with two members of the old Manson gang. Both of these women had discovered Jesus, rather conveniently, some years before parole hearings. Now they were shopping around for a publisher to get the word out. My publisher friend had turned them down. "You've got to have at least some ethical standards," he said. "But other companies will be standing in line." What we are seeing in our generation, he added, is the logical conclusion to the previous generation's over-emphasis on speaking about God. The word "testimony" has become totally divorced from its action-oriented meaning in the Christian tradition. No wonder our generation finds little solace or hope in the prevailing religious over-kill!

Everytime I return from a preacher's convention or walk out of a religious bookstore, I can empathize with Mary Magdalene at the empty tomb. You will remember the angels saw her weeping and asked why and she responded, "Because they have taken my Lord, and I do not know where they have laid him." In a time when "bearing witness to Christ" has become associated with verbal diarrhea, I sometimes feel that "They have taken away my Lord and I do not know where they have laid him." Religious perception can become buried under a mountain of words. A great deal of the quality of our faith is rapidly declining due to the fact that the language of the faith is becoming devalued. *As Christians we have an important responsibility with respect to words.*

In the Old Testament much is written about the speech of God. In Hebrew thought words possessed the quality of a magic spell. Once uttered a word took on a life of its own beyond the control of the speaker. For example, when Jacob tricked Isaac into blessing him instead of his brother Esau, nothing could be done. The words had been set loose. And the authors of Genesis contend that God spoke and the earth was created. God said "Let there be... and there it was." Words were believed to change things in and of themselves.

Now the New Testament moved away from that perspective into a more amazing claim: "The word became flesh." *All of the talk became activity.* A person lived out what theretofore had only been talked about. And he left a new thought: "people will know you by your love." Even when he performed miracles of healing and the recipients wanted to run around testifying what had happened, Jesus told them, "go home and the people will see me."

Jesus never intended for talk about God to replace living for God. Words were always intended to *evoke actions.* Words themselves never made a life powerful.

Witness Jesus' style of living. In the New Testament very few of Jesus' prayers are preserved. You see, Jesus most often prayed alone. His prayers were not pompous public displays but private utterances of thanks. In fact, the model prayer which he left us, the Lord's Prayer, contains only 66 words. *Prayed slowly, the Lord's Prayer takes but 22 seconds!* More astounding is the fact if we take all of the original words of Jesus we have preserved for us in the New Testament and speak them into a recorder we will find the tape runs no more than 38 minutes! Thirty eight minutes of verbal testimony preserved from an entire life - Jesus possessed the ability to get to the heart of the matter without a great deal of verbage. *Jesus' life made his words powerful.* He did not depend on his words to make his life powerful. And he held out the same style to us: "Not everyone who cries Lord, Lord, will enter the kingdom, only those who do the will of the Father."

The early Christian church understood that perspective well. When those small groups of people worshiped together, often in secret, their order of service was similar to most churches' order of service today – with one important addition. As they met, they read the scriptures (usually the Psalms), took communion, and then went around the room, one by one, for verbal self-disclosure and confession of their shortcomings. Then they had prayers of forgiveness. Then they went around the room again and each and every Christian had to tell orally the plans of action they would follow in the coming week to make restitution for their faults and shortcomings. A period of fellowship then concluded their meeting.

You can readily ascertain what was different. The early church did more than pray and confess. You had to come clean with your plan of action for doing something about your talk. Those early Christians knew actions did more for their stability than all the platitudes they could utter, prayers they could pray, or beliefs they could articulate. *Words themselves were held in very low regard.*

Jesus, Paul and most of the great figures in our own land have been people of great influence but few words. The apostle Paul lacked the physical attractiveness that could have given him an edge in public speaking. One day Paul was going to visit a church where he had never been before, so a member of the church wrote someone who knew Paul well and asked him to describe Paul so that the church would recognize him. The letter described Paul as "bald-headed, with a big nose, a squatty build, and an unattractive face. His utterance was not very strong and his syntax was horrible. In addition, his personality defects were so numerous that he could get along with no one."

You wonder how a person like that could be such a builder of churches. But if you look closely, you realize that Paul had *one of the most attractive inner beings there ever was.* What distinguished him were two things: 1) He had a profound love for people that manifested itself in actions. He would do anything for you. He was like Jesus in that regard: if he thought washing a person's feet or shining their shoes would bring them to God, he would do it.

He had a profound love for people.

2) *He possessed an unshakable confidence in the divine purposes of God coming to pass.* He gave it all he had, never 10 percent. He would travel the world over to build up a church. He'd been shipwrecked so many times and thrown in prison so many times that he had lost count. He possessed an unshakable confidence in the divine purposes of God coming to pass.

Paul could only do a few things but he did those to the utmost of his capability. Such is always more effective than talking at length about a great many things and doing little.

We need that kind of influential living in our world of *words.* We need people who by their examples teach us how to live. *Most great achievements have been achieved by those who exercised economy in language but put forth greatness in effort.*

The formation of our own country evidences this reality. After Benjamin Franklin returned all the way from France to sign the Declaration of Independence, Thomas Jefferson wrote these words to a friend: "I served with General George Washington in the legislature of Virginia before the revolution and during it with Dr. Ben Franklin in Congress. I never heard either of them speak ten minutes at a time ... They never spoke to anything except the main point which was to decide the question. They laid their shoulders to the great points knowing that the little ones would follow of themselves."

Now those are the kind of people you can hitch your future to -- they never talked more than ten minutes at a time but one would travel the world over if it would serve his friends and the other would stand knee deep in snow all night with little clothing if it would serve his friends. When they spoke, everybody listened.

In this multi-media age of skimmed surfaces and easy confidence, that reality is whatever can be heard and taped and reported, we must have more than words to place our hope in. Words by themselves will not educate our children into a hope in God. Words by themselves will not bring hope to the stranger. Words by themselves will not provide a hope to energize the lethargic. The whole world waits for the words to become flesh, for the lives to make the words powerful.

In this respect the Christian church, as a community of service and intention, can help us find the discipline we need to turn prom ise into reality.

Part Two

The Service of Hope

6

Hope That Comes From Discipline

The nation of India has contributed a Sanskrit story which tells our story. It seems that four royal sons were given the freedom by their parents to go anywhere and master anything. So the four brothers said to one another, "Let us search the earth and learn a special science." After deciding this, they agreed on a place where they would meet again some years later. So they started off, each in a different direction to learn a specialty and make a name for themselves. The time passed, and came the day when the brothers agreed to meet again in the appointed place. After 10 years, they were all together again and they began to ask one another what they had learned. "I have mastered a science," said the first," which makes it possible for me, if I have nothing but a piece of bone of some creature, to create straightway the flesh that goes with it." "I", said the second," have made a name for myself, by knowing how to grow a creature's skin and hair, if some-one gives me bones with flesh on them." The third brother, became very excited and spoke up — "Wonderful. I have learned how to create limbs if I have the flesh, the skin and the hair." The fourth brother could hardly control his ecstasy. "And I," concluded the fourth brother," know how to give life to any dead creature if its form is complete with limbs."

Thereupon the four brothers went into the jungle to find some bones so that they could demonstrate their specialties. As fate would have it, the bones they found were the bones of a lion. But they did not know that. So they picked up the bones. One added flesh to the bones, the second grew hide and hair, the third com-pleted it with matching limbs, and the fourth gave the lion life. Shaking its heavy name, the ferocious beast arose with its menacing mouth, sharp teeth and merciless claws and jumped on its creators. The lion killed them all and vanished contentedly into the jungle!

That poignant story always reminds me of the fact that every successful, good, and free expression in our lives holds the potential to destroy us, *unless we set our freedom squarely within the boundaries of some outside guidance*. Even the good elements we create must be controlled or they will leap on us and kill us. History over and over again demonstrates that *freedom without discipline can end in personal chaos and social anarchy*.

Religion itself must be controlled. In fact over a third of the beds in our country's mental hospitals are occupied by poor, suffering individuals who cannot control their religions. But the churches and the seal of baptism are old and respected guideposts. In a world in which allegiance to material gods, subscription to inhumane philsophies, and mesmerization by illusion-making psychologies have swept most of our guideposts away, there is at least some moral consistency in having the 10 Commandments, the Sermon on the Mount, and the Lord's Prayer to guide you as you start picking up the world's bones.

I suppose that for all of us, there is some confrontation from someone, behind the beginning of our Christian pilgrimage. I remember Frank Broyles, the former coach at the University of Arkansas, telling me that he was glad his mother made him come to church until he was old enough to understand why.

All of us need to acknowledge the need for discipline for our good intentions. Jesus certainly did. Addressing the religious leaders of his day, Jesus said in John's gospel: *"But if you do not believe what Moses wrote, how are you to believe what I say?"* (John 5:46-47). In other words, if you don't have the tough discipline of the 10 commandments behind you, how can you understand which of your good intentions to follow?

These are rather startling words — the freedom of Jesus demands the discipline of Moses and the 10 Commandments. I say startling because in the face of the love of Jesus, the list of "Thou shalt nots" seems rather out of joint. In fact, had a certain party won its point in the formation of the early church, the discipline of the law, along with the whole Old Testament would have been eliminated from the Bible. This party thought that the new religion of Jesus freed us up from all those Old Testament rules. But here is Jesus saying, "if you do not believe what Moses wrote, how are you to believe what I say?"

I must admit freedom always makes better copy than responsibility. Consider the great and glorious music of Handel's Oratorio "Israel in Egypt." The whole epoch event is depicted as a freedom movement, a liberation movement and Handel's music is a freedom song. Handel does not write of the context of the law and the covenant.

But Jesus knew that love and freedom have to have some toughness in them. Even love has to be controlled. Some of the most horrible things on the face of this earth are done in the name of love and freedom. Sometimes even love must be confrontive and demand that people see themselves for what they really are. *It would not be an act of love to watch the four royal brothers find their bones and support them in their efforts when you know that the product of their creation can destroy them.* In fact to merely compliment them on their success would be a sin.

There is no greater hopelessness than the feeling of operating in life without effective outside guidance.

At some point, when the road being traveled is one which leads to disaster, it is an act of love to confront the loved one with what is really going on.

This is not so easy as it seems. Much of religion in our world has become shallow and manipulative. In order to attract great crowds some churches have cut their conscience and their integrity to fit this year's social fashions. And it works. Because more and more people shop for churches in the way they shop for food brands — according to personal taste, social position, and economic resources. *Yet these privatized values provide neither the base nor the tough discipline for people to mature or to fashion a just society.*

Producing a disciplined approach to life is hard even for a church. Maybe especially hard for a church. You see, churches are especially enamored with *nursing* syndromes. We sometimes want to define love as taking care of others, propping them up, and fulfilling their wants. Yet pouring oil on wounds and soothing hurts are not always expressions of love if such does not lead to maturity.

Jesus the Christ became an instrument of God's love and hope to the world. That love and that hope were not always sweet and soothing. jesus possessed the ability to confront people with themselves and set boundaries, a very necessary part of establishing human hope.

The fifth chapter of John's gospel contains an account of a lame man who had been lying by the pool of Bethzatha for thirty-eight years. For thirty-eight years, this man had been supported by his friends. Faithfully and laboriously, for thirty-eight years, his friends had "loved" him in the manner in which they understood love, and given him "hope" as they had understood hope. They nursed him along in his lameness and carried him to a pool where rumor had it that an angel stirred the waters. The pool at Bethzatha was fed by underground streams. When some of the streams became intermittenly activated, a bubbling effect took place. In that superstitious society, it was felt that whoever got in first would be healed.

Year after year this man sat there, waiting for a miracle — just one more step, one more stirring, one more angel, one more fall into the pool and perhaps he could find happiness.

He was reaching out for the only kind of hope he knew. Then one day the Christ appeared on the scene and asked the man a question which none of the man's friends had apparently asked: *"Do you want to be healed?*

How unusual and inappropriate that question sounds. Why ask a man who had sought healing for thirty-eight years if he really wanted to be healed? But Jesus had a way of telling the truth. *Here was a lame person who had grown dependent on his friends and his superstitions.* He had joined countless others in hanging around a certain spot looking for something to happen. His happiness depended on achieving a goal that was always a little bit beyond his reach! Jesus *confronted* the man: "Do you *really want* to be healed?"

Jesus called the man to a certain kind of disciplined accountability for himself. The man had to recover his confidence in himself and in his heritage instead of resting his happiness on blind hopes for a miracle. He had good intentions. For thirty-eight years he had good intentions. But after a period of being lame and leaning over backwards on his friends, his personal integrity and all of his respected guideposts had slipped away. He gave his allegiance to false gods; he subscribed to inhumane practices, and mesmerized by illusion, he turned to superstition. In his desperation to find something that would work, he simply picked up the wrong religious bones.

Jesus called the man to add self-discipline and discernment to his good intentions. "Get up. Rise. Move away from here. Take up your bed and walk. Be responsible for yourself." *The healing of Christ is never gained apart from personal responsibility.*

You and I seek hope in the midst of a complex world of many life style options. And in looking for simple answers we often make simple mistakes. One of those simple mistakes of enormous consequence is to think that freedom and order have nothing to do with each other. Order yields to freedom we think, for in our simple-minded ways, order is repressive and freedom is expressive. But *what is our attitude toward order when freedom no longer appears to work?* To wrestle with life seriously is to recognize that we need help beyond our own. We need discipline for our own good intentions. That is one reason we have churches. We are not the first people to experience human life as a mosaic of failure and achievement, frustration and satisfaction, misery and grandeur; we are not the first to face unpredictability; we are not the first to know the fewness of our days. There is a heritage of countless Christians before our birth and the reality of contemporary friends, who remind us that there is a high code to live by, a healing for our lamenesses and a freedom greater than any freedom the world can offer.

7

Hope Empowered by Commitment

Many people no longer believe that commitment to a task can pay off. Our American culture appears to be perilously close to losing its incentive for hard work. Many people today are not prepared to tolerate adverse conditions, hard work, and self-sacrifice for future rewards. We want it all and we want it all right now. We live in an "instant culture": instant foods; instant celebrities; instant cures; instant pleasures; instant creation of life; and instant obsolescence of not only products but ideas, computer systems and even whole communities. We have even reached the point where the USFL sold its games to two major TV networks even though the league had no teams, no coaches, no uniforms and no players.

Many people, especially youth, believe that benefits accrue instantly to the most talented and not over the long-run to the most committed. In 1967, 69% of the youth in this country answered "yes" to the question: "Does hard work always pay off?" But by 1975, only 25% (one in four) of American students answered "yes" to the same question. This view of work probably reflects attitudes in their homes as well.

Small wonder that hope is the rarest item to be found in our contemporary society. At the appearance of the first closed door, many people give up.

Such perceived attitudes trouble me. So I wish to tell you about the most productive and fruitful individual I have ever met. His name is Jack and he came into my life in a most unusual way.[6] On a crisp fall day I had completed hospital calls to church members in Anderson, South Carolina. When I reached the hospital parking lot, I felt a hand on my shoulder. There behind me stood a member of my church with a rather beleaguered-looking young woman whom I had never seen before. The distraught woman explained that her husband had just returned from surgery. The family had not been to church in years but this latest surgery had awakened feelings of need in her husband and he wanted to talk with me about God.

As we walked back toward the hospital, Jack's wife explained the situation. Jack was 32 years old. His I.Q. hovered near 150. He had been an extremely talented man who had breezed his way through M. I. T. at an early age. His high energy level could not be totally absorbed by his professional work as a computer manager for an oil company so as a hobby at age 25 he built his own race car, which he subsequently qualified in the Indianapolis 500. At that time in his life, Jack began to be bothered with equilibrium problems and a doctor's checkup confirmed multiple sclerosis. Realizing that his body would quickly deteriorate, the doctor suggested that Jack, his wife, and little boy leave New England and move to a warmer climate. But as soon as they arrived in South Carolina, an examination discovered that Jack also had terminal cancer. He was given only a short time to live. That's the person I was asked to visit.

I entered the dimly lit hospital room with caution. A frail body painfully turned itself in my direction. Without any introduction he said, "I want to become involved in your church, where is it?" I told him, and he said, "I have no talent or money left, but I will be committed. You can count on me; I'll work hard."

I simply sat in amazed silence. Here was a 32 year old man with both multiple sclerosis and cancer. He had no use of his arms or legs. He had less than normal vision; he saw only flickering images at times. And his finances had been totally depleted by the costs of his treatments. All talent had been stripped away. But he promised to be committed. Such apparently misguided hope fascinated me.

I'll never forget the first Sunday Jack came to church. It was raining. So his wife drove the car up on the grass and parked at the steps of the sanctuary. She put his wheelchair at the bottom of the steps and honked the car horn until the ushers came outside to help. The noise made quite a disruption in the service. Consequently several ushers were thereafter assigned to always remain outside in anticipation of his arrival. Week after week, Jack doggedly kept coming. He had to sit in a special chair with pillows strapped to it in the back of the sanctuary but that didn't seem to bother him.

As time passed, Jack's presence every Sunday produced some remarkable changes in the church. People who had not attended the service in years because of their physical handicaps began to appear regularly in their wheelchairs and walkers. Others who had stayed away because of personal and/or emotional difficulties also returned. The stranger was setting an example that raised the expectations of an entire congregation as to what a human being can and cannot do. People who had felt little hope operating in their lives in many years began to suddenly find a way to give meaning to their physical condition.

Jack's presence also redirected our long-range building plans. For years the church had existed without a sufficient recreation and fellowship hall. But when the time finally arrived to develop designs for a new building, a new idea emerged. The sanctuary needed to be remodeled and expanded to provide ramps, corridors, and seating to accommodate the increased numbers of people. Soon we were engaged in that project. Jack would arrive early in the morning at least once a week and lie on a cot in the back of a station wagon, giving the builder and architect detailed advice on wheelchair access, visual effects, and physical placement of items.

Having helped improve our attitudes and our buildings, Jack next sought to contribute to our worship. As the multiple sclerosis began to take away more of his vision, he looked for new ways to feed his inquisitive mind. So he ordered recordings of theology books from the Library of Congress. From listening to these books he would extract sermon ideas and quotations and peck them out with a rod stuck between his teeth on his typewriter. Then he had them mailed to me for my sermon files.

One day the inevitable happened. His body simply deteriorated and he had to be transferred to a special nursing home a hundred miles away. I assumed that at last the curtain had come down. But one day the head nurse from that institution called me. Jack's wife had read the church newsletter to him. And he had discovered that communion was to be celebrated the next Sunday. Jack asked the nurse to see if one of our deacons would bring communion to him. He wanted to take communion with *his* church as an extension of its worship in addition to knowing the chaplain of the nursing home. So each communion Sunday after that a small group of deacons drove the hundred miles to carry Jack's communion to him. Soon the other shut-in and hospitalized church members heard of this and they began to make similar requests. It became necessary to organize many people to fan out over the entire county to serve these people on communion Sunday. The effort energized the entire congregation.

Our church was revolutionized by a stranger who had no money and could not use his arms, his legs, or his eyes. *All he had to offer was commitment.*

I share this admittedly long, personal story with you because at times all of us are tempted to believe the problems with our economy, our labor, our churches, our personal lives and our country lie beyond our control because of a lack of resources. Resources and talent are not needed items. *Commitment is always worth more than talent.* The heroes of our Scriptures did not succeed because of superior talent. Most of them were people who had a little real talent to turn over to God. They simply offered their commitments. *Not the big shots but the sure shots have made up the kingdom of God.*

In terms of innovation and theological expression, I'm not certain how talented even Jesus was. He apparently quoted from the Old Testament more than he authored original material. In fact 81 verses out of the 111 verses in the sermon on the mount were straight out of the Old Testament. And was their every a punier audience than the dozen people who listened to that sermon on the mount? Peter was a loudmouth who believed in winning. But when things went bad, he went to pieces. Nathaniel was a bigot. If you didn't come from the same place he came from, he thought you were no good. And look at the total overview of the makeup of the people Jesus worked with — the Roman officer, the sick old lady, the crazy man who lived in the cemetery, the over-enthusiastic scribe, the terrified disciples, and the lunatic. *What unlikely looking heroes.* Far from perfect. But Jesus, while he didn't author much new material, sought a new ideal as to how close one can get to God and *how committed one can be to a power greater than any power.* The New Testament records over and over that the early Christian church was far from perfect in its life together. *But they committed all things in common.* They affirmed commitment over talent and intimacy over resource.

The first time Jesus laid eyes on Simon, he told him that from then on he'd call him Peter, which is Greek for *rock*. Now a rock isn't the prettiest thing in creation or the fanciest or the smartest, and if it gets rolling in the wrong direction, watch out. But there is no nonsense about a rock. And once it settles down, it's pretty much there to stay. Barring earthquakes you can depend on it about as much as you can depend on anything. So Jesus called him The Rock and it stuck with him the rest of his life. And he stuck with Jesus the rest of *his* life.[7]

Hard work can accomplish a great many things in both labor and religion that dormant talent will never do. Our problem in this country is not a lack of talent and resources. It's lack of commitment.

Commitment has a strange way of revitalizing both the committed person and those who come into contact with that person. It takes only a few totally committed people to energize and totally turn-around an entire institution.

In the fourth chapter of John's gospel is the dramatic story of Jesus' encounter with a Samaritan woman beside Jacob's well. The story depicts an incredible change which took place in the life of the woman. But equally amazing is the assertion that a change took place in the life of Jesus.

The woman is pictured as one who slowly dragged herself out to the well at noonday. She did this because she wanted to avoid contact with other women. She was depressed, ashamed, tired and beaten down. Life had not been very fulfilling. Her hopes had evaporated. But in the course of a few short minutes her whole world-view was turned upside down. She became committed to something greater than herself. She exuberantly ran into the village and openly sought out her peers to let them in on the change in her life. The before-and-after contrast is a remarkable spectacle.

But notice also the effect that the woman's commitment had on Jesus' hopes. Jesus came to the well exhausted. He was weary from his journey and work and plopped down on the well while the disciples went to get him something to eat. Then a woman came along and Jesus went to work with her. But instead of becoming more exhausted he became refreshed. When his disciples returned Jesus was not even hungry anymore. His work and seeing the woman become committed to God, put more back into him than it took out of him.

Work ought to be like that. Church ought to be like that. That's the secret of revitalization. Commitment to a cause has the ability to add to us as well as take from us. Our work can become like food, *if it is our love and hope made visible.*

8

Hope That Moves Beyond Mere Adoration

A few years ago I accepted an invitation to be the preacher in a Good Friday service sponsored by the downtown churches of Knoxville, Tennessee. The service was held in a huge Episcopal church. So on the appointed day I flew into Knoxville, Tennessee, and had my brother-in-law meet me at the airport. He drove me to the church. I called the host minister to inform him of my arrival and received directions to the robing room. Since I still had a full thirty minutes before the service began, I stood out on a street corner a few blocks from the church, talking with some fellow-clergy and watching at a distance as people walked into the church for our service.

Then a young woman in great agitation came running down the street toward us. "Mr. Warlick," she screamed, "where have you been?" This puzzled me. "Right here," I responded. "There's still plenty of time before the service."

"Didn't anyone tell you the service is televised live?" I shook my head. "The make-up man is beside himself. There's nothing he can do now but a few brush-ons."

So, I followed this woman, listened to the heavy cursing of her station's make-up man, and finally put on my robe. At precisely twelve noon they led me to a seat beneath an elevated pulpit with a staircase leading up to it. Surrounding the pulpit in a semi-circle were a battery of television spotlights. And hanging down from the ceiling above where the congregation sat was another row of powerful spotlights. I could not see three feet past my nose. When I stepped into that pulpit I stared into an ocean of bright lights. I could not see the face of a single person in the congregation. Instead of speaking to faces, I felt as if my words were falling over the edge of the pulpit and down to the floor. There were no faces to remind me of the loyalties, life-styles and struggles which compose human existence.

Then, as soon as the sermon ended and the last hymn had begun, someone from the television station led me through a back door for a cup of coffee and that was that. For all I knew I could have been preaching to an audience of nudists. Now, amazingly enough I received a number of letters following the event from people telling me what a marvelous service it was. They *adored* the sermon and I think we probably did a fairly good job of admiring Jesus and his death on the cross.

But I could not experience true worship just being an admirer of Jesus. Worship is possible when you are united with people with whom you are bound together in ways of trust, hope and shared loyalty.

Christian hope is much more than admiring Jesus. To be a Christian involves more than expressing how attached we are to the memory of Jesus. Jesus points to a living God. Therein is our hope. Tell me Jesus is only a god of bright lights to be adored and worshipped and most of the hope for our age is gone. But tell me Jesus has opened the door to a power that can come into my life and I have something I can participate in and hope for.

Jesus came to open the gates to a new age and to deal with real people. *He shunned the worship and the admiration of his followers.* Instead, he wanted us to walk through the gates that he had opened for us. He refused to accept titles of greatness, even to the point of asking, "why do you call me great?" He satirized those who wear fancy robes and process in kingly fashion in parades. He told his disciples they would do even mightier works than he had done. He also stated that the lowest member of heaven was as great as John the Baptist. In John's gospel it is articulated that this light in the darkness, this Jesus who dwelt with God, would give everyone the power to become children of God.

Why did Jesus shun the admiration of his followers?

Let me share with you an illustration of what can happen when a pioneer becomes worshipped and admired rather than believed in and worked with.[8] For generations, perhaps centuries, human beings tried to run a timed mile in four minutes. But none ever did. The magic four minute mark stood as the ultimate goal. As long as distances had been measured and clocked, no one ever ran that fast. Then, one day a man named Roger Bannister put forth a tremendous effort. With unbelievable courage, extraordinary drive, abiding hope, and immense personal power, he cracked that magic barrier. He ran a mile in less than four minutes. It made Bannister's name a household word. But amazingly, *within six months after Bannister's epic run, at least four other individuals ran the mile in less than four minutes.* Why should it be that for as long as humans had attempted the clocked mile, over seventy-five years, no one had ever run a four-minute mile — yet when a person finally achieved it, so many made the same achievement within six months? The answer is obvious. Humankind had placed a psychological ceiling on what the mile could be run in. One person raised that ceiling, expanded hope and ushered in a new age. Within six months at least four other people walked through the gates he opened. Today a mile run is not considered a good race unless several of the competitors break four minutes.

Let's conjecture a change in the course of history. Suppose that when Bannister clocked his four minute mile, athletes proclaimed him a once-in-a-lifetime runner. "No one can hope to be like Bannister. He was perfect. It's blasphemy to try to be like him." Suppose they built a shrine out of the track where that "once-in-eternity" event took place and little shrines popped up all over the country where people could come and read accounts of how Bannister ran the epic mile. Suppose young athletes, instead of catching his spirit and training hard to do what he had done, became content to quote verses from Bannister's biography. Suppose people quit trying to stretch through the gates he had opened and instead put their effort into keeping his admiration at a high pitch. We know what would have happened. Bannister would have been the *only* person to have ever run a four minute mile. Instead of a pioneer opening a new age, we would have a god being *adored* by millions, studied by scholars, and supported by a few track fans making small pledges of money to keep his memory alive.

Do we fully understand the implications of God sending his only son to be the pioneer of a new age in which all men and women were invited to participate? You see, *humans had placed a psychological ceiling on God's love for and presence with his people.* Their hope was at a low ebb. The legalism of Judaism, the ethical deterioration in the promised land and the ugliness of human prejudice had created a psychological ceiling concerning how close a person could hope to get to God. So God opened the gates to a new era. He sent his son to love and to relate to men and women as never before. He lifted the ceiling on love. He stated that all of us could run the race of life and live it more abundantly and that we could become sons and daughters of God. He raised the ceiling and thousands walked in under it. The gates were flung wide open to the kingdom of God. The pioneer intended we should break some bread and drink some wine or grape juice, remembering what he had done, and share in the power and hope he had turned loose on the world.

But alas, after decades, men and women began to slowly close those gates he had flung open. The ceiling was lowered again. People began to admire Jesus and adore his memory. They memorized his life instead of looking for *his power* in their own life. They began to say "no one can hope to be like him. It's blasphemy to try." They had little visions and set small goals for themselves. They made salvation copyright and wrapped him up in stained glass. They even set his life to music. They made him the most *admired* instead of emulated leader in the world. *He became an absolute to be idolized instead of a power and a hope to be daily reckoned with.*

It's obvious that Jesus feared this. Jesus lived in a world and among a people who put great store by holy writings. Some Saturday night when I'm working at the church, I stand in the parking lot and watch the Jewish people in the synagogue across the street. The procession of the Torah, the holy writings, is an inspiring sight. The Jewish people always have put great store in their holy writings. Now isn't it curious that Jesus, as God's son, never wrote anything? Jeremiah wrote God's words. He even had a secretary to jot them down so he could have them. Paul wrote dozens of long epistles to churches. But Jesus apparently never took care to write anything down. Nothing autobiographical. Not even a personal note. On one occasion he scribbled in the sand, when the adulterous woman was brought to him. But he wiped that out before anyone could see what he had written. Apparently Jesus did not want to leave anything written down that people could idolize instead of catching his spirit and hope after he was gone! Jesus viewed his life as a liberating force and not as a graven image to worship.

Perhaps the most critical issue facing us as individuals and as a people is this: can we walk through the gates Jesus has opened? We have a great hope available to us. We can admire it. We can adore it. We can even fill out a pledge card and invite a few people to come to church and sacrifice some hours this year to its well being. All of that we will do in accordance to the psychological ceiling we have placed on our lives with Christ.

But if we ever take his ethics as our ethics, his dictates as our dictates, his mission as our mission, his hope as our hope, his kingdom as our kingdom, our ambitions will be far higher than they are now!

Men and women since antiquity have wrestled with the question, "what does God want from us?" Certainly God wants more than our admiration. Apparently the problem of adoring and admiring God under a psychological ceiling of hope has been a concern of Christianity for a very long time. The book of James concerns itself with that problem. Finally, in exasperation, James comments that admiration without a life fixed to deeds is as lifeless as a corpse. He even evidences Rahab the harlot as someone justified by God through letting the power and hope of God get into her life.

As we think about the fatalism and pessimism in our nuclear and technological age, it is apparent that a God merely to be admired is hardly sufficient for the challenges which confront us. We can admire and adore what has been done for us in the life of Christ. But that hope and power which fueled his life, that desire to see God's will done on earth as well as in heaven, must get into our lives, our businesses, our personal ambitions, and our visions for the future. Our response to life can be no higher than the psychological ceiling we have placed on God's ability to use us for powerful acts of goodness and love. We can do no more than we believe we are. We can have hope only in direct proportion to our acceptance of God's offer of sonship or daughtership. But if we can envision Christ as the pioneer of a new age, we can embrace both the visible and invisible dimensions of hope. We, too, can learn to have faith in the unseen. We, too, can become starters or pioneers for the age which will come on earth as in heaven.

9

Hope in Things Seen and Unseen

Several years ago a teacher in San Francisco, California, did a study with her students. Children of the same age from both deprived economic situations and from stable economic situation were asked "would you rather have a penny lollipop right now or an ice cream sundae tomorrow?" Almost all the children from low economic backgrounds raised their hands for the lollipop now. Almost all of the children from families of economic stability raised their hands for the sundae later. Even at an early age, the survivalist mentality prohibited some children from acting in their own best interests.

It is an indication of the impoverished state of religion in our society that so many people, especially young people, are operating on a very dangerous "give-it-to-me-now" syndrome relative to church. The need for instant gratification is so great that many of us are raising our hands for lollipop religion because it looks good now. I see it in people who are drawn only to the most stable and developed circumstances, in youth who demand the group have 100 teenagers in it before they think it has meaning, and in adults who hold a low opinion of something because it isn't an already finished product. *I maintain that such a mentality prohibits some people from acting in their own best interest when it comes to their future happiness.* We become enfeebled when we lose our ability to start something and dream dreams. Consequently we wind up in later life with a fistful of lollipops when we could have had so much more out of our faith and church experiences *had we cultivated the ability to embrace the unseen. I think the ability to embrace and have faith in the unseen is the most important thing a parent can teach a child and even the most im-*

portant thing an adult can learn to do.

When I was a teenager in South Carolina, much of my time was spent participating in my high school's football program. Now in my era, two of our outstanding athletes were named Warren and Ricky. Warren was a year older than Ricky and he played directly in front of Ricky on defense. Warren was a steady, unflamboyant athlete who always managed to get a hand on the ball carrier when the play came in his direction. He made the initial contact on almost every charge toward him. Now Ricky was one of the world's best at lowering the boom once Warren had hit the ball carrier and stood him up. Ricky would pile on top of a stumbling ball carrier with a crash you could hear in the stands. Warren made a few all-conference teams while Ricky was all-everything, with college scouts hanging around him after most games. Warren finally graduated and went off to college. Mid-way through the next season, Ricky quit the team and never played another play of football. Ever! You see, all of his career he had never had to do anything except finish off what the man in front of him had started. And *it was too late for him to learn how to start being unselfish.* He never learned how to initiate the play himself. He became a disciplinary problem and finally quit the effort altogether. Learning to be an initiator is so much more difficult for one who has only been a beneficiary.

I related this to you because I think it evidences a truth which holds the key to understanding life and the secret of happiness. Psychoanalyst Erik Erikson has often called us to reaffirm the cycle of generations. He has noted that our psychosocial survival is safeguarded only by vital virtues which develop in the interplay of successive and overlapping generations. Our Christian life-style must cogwheel with the stages of others who came long before us and with others who will be born long after our death. *In other words, we must not only finish what others have started, we must also learn how to start what others will finish for us.* A message I read on a sign in Rochester, New York, in this regard, seems to me to be a sure-fire key to happiness. *"Dedicate yourself to a cause which will go on after your life ends."* Most of the truly great people in our world have been people ahead of their time. Knowing that they may not live to see the triumph of the cause they stood for, they nevertheless set down their faith and lived by it. They appealed not to the past or even the present, but to the future for their vindication. *They knew how to be starters and they knew that God is Lord of history.* They trusted in humankind. They understood full well what Jesus meant when he said unto Thomas, "You have believed because you have seen me; blessed are the people who have not seen and *yet* have believed."

Those who act on their beliefs are not blind optimists. Far from it. They are the realists in our kind of world. Leonardo da Vinci, almost 500 years ago, foresaw airplanes, drew pictures of them, and put them in a book. The impatient critics must have laughed his faith to scorn. "Let it come, now", Leonardo, "and let us see it. Or we won't join in." Well, after five centuries, Leonardo has been vindicated. He was the realist. He was a starter. Others completed the work. But Leonardo's hope sustained him.

Our cause and effect, gratification-seeking world has a hard time understanding such things. Yet the God of history embraces more than our little generation. God is God in the long-run.

Most of the positive elements in my life were started by people who never got to see the fruits of their labors. My religion owes so much to a man named Moses who left everything he possessed to go to Egypt and rally a group of slaves. In their behalf he argued before Pharoah. For forty years he kept them together as they wandered in the desert. He encouraged them. He coaxed them. He interpreted to them a covenant with God by which they became a nation. Probably no person in history gave as much time and energy to one project as Moses did trying to get Israel into the promised land. Yet Moses died without ever seeing the payoff. That privilege was accorded his descendants. Moses had started the vision. He had found his place in the universe. Moses was a *starter.* His hope sustained him.

Another contributor to Christianity was the second Isaiah. Isaiah studied the scriptures he had and embraced God's revelation in the world around him. For him God was the God of *all* people and not just the Jews. He believed that one day a man would be born who would deepen that revelation. Such a man would lead to a new understanding of God which would include non-Jews. His name would be called mighty counselor, The Prince of Peace. Yet Isaiah died hundreds of years before anyone saw that belief become flesh in the life of Jesus of Nazareth. Isaiah was a *starter.* His hope sustained him.

An unseen contributor to my educational life was my mother.

We children became aware of an underlying intention in the family that we should be educated in a way beyond what our parents had been privileged to have. My sister and I were stimulated through cooperating with a purpose greater than our own. We would never have gotten anywhere without that. My mother wanted me to someday, for however a brief a period, teach in a seminary. She died ten days before I was appointed a professor at Harvard. She never got to see it.

Often it's that way. Richard Furman in 1780 looked around him and saw in South Carolina and North Carolina that most of the people were unable to read and write. His influence for education led to the Furman Academy and Theological Institute in Edgefield, South Carolina. Later they became Furman University and Southern Baptist Theological Seminary. But Richard Furman died before the institution bearing his name ever opened its doors. He was a starter. But his hope sustained him.

And consider those who worked so hard to get your church founded and off the ground who died before they ever got to see it. They were all starters.

But *never cry for starters, my friends*. Starters are the happiest people in the world. They grasp the concept of the whole life — that the cycle of one generation continues itself into the next. So what if they never saw the end product, the effort was more than justified. The vision of what might be made them all better people than they ever would have been had they been called upon only to tread water or finish another's beginning. Visions of home, church, and a thousand other things gave them a place in the universe. If necessary their dreams could be the unbroken chain of dedicated human loyalty and vision. It's a strange peace when you realize God is Lord of History.

No, my friends, never weep for starters, for those who have faith in the unseen. Weep only for those who never have that privilege. Perhaps the most critical need for an embracement of the unseen lies in the realm of living for peace in a world of violence. Nowhere else is there such a desperate need for Christian affirmation of the Lordship of Christ. How can we find the motivation and understanding for pioneering an age of peace when we are confronted with so much violence?

Is not the dilemma of modern belief our inability to reconcile our cherished notions of peace and love with the uncherished facts about evil and violence in our world? War is such a hopeless enter-prise. It flies in the face of Christian optimism about human ex-istence. When cherished hopes for peace wind up in the valley of physical violence, the Christian encounters an emotional as well as intellectual dilemma. And since the evening news on television can bring war into our dens and bedrooms, the reconciliation of cherished notions with uncherished facts seems to be essential for human hope in Christian possibilities.

10

Living for Peace: the Hopeful Alternative

The Beatitudes of Jesus are the best teachings in the world. The notions are cherished: peacemaking, meekness, righteousness, etc. All of us hold to those high ideals of what human beings should be like. But human beings are not that way. The reality of sin is everywhere.

So where does that leave us? According to Jesus, you and I are to be peacemakers. Jesus is quite clear about that. A Christian is one who believes in peace. No other Savior died on a cross asking God to forgive the very people who killed him. Even the enemies of Christ recognized that *ours is a religion of peace*. For this very reason Adolph Hitler often lamented Germany's reliance on Christianity. In his memoirs, Albert Speer, Hitler's architect, commented that Hitler believed Germany was unfortunate in being saddled with this religion of meekness and flabbiness. In fact, he often remarked, "Why didn't we have the religion of the Japanese, who regard sacrifice for the fatherland as the highest good . . . or the Mohammedans, for theirs is a religion that believes in spreading the faith by the sword and subjugating all nations to that faith . . .?"

Virtually the whole world realizes Christian people and Christian nations cherish the notion of peace. But cherished notions seem always to run headlong into the uncherished facts of human sin. A syndicated critic of the last century, Ambrose Bierce,[9] had enough of the unreality of cherished notions. So he attemped to write a series of modern fables in which Aesop was brought up to date to fit the rough and tumble world. Remember the parable of the mouse and the lion? Bierce tells it as follows. A lion encountered a mouse ensnared in a trap in the jungle. The lion was about to swat the mouse when the mouse remonstrated, "Sir, please release me, for I would do the same for you should you be found in a similar dilemma." The lion was impressed with the verbal mouse. He released the mouse and both went on their separate ways. Some days later, the mouse was passing along when he heard great growls in the underbush. He found the same lion with his paw caught in an enormous trap and unable to move. Greeting one another, the mouse then proceeded to gnaw off the lion's tail.

Sometimes I feel that the United States is like a powerful lion in a world of many up and coming mice and a few other powerful lions. And every time we give in to our cherished notions and help some of these mice out of their economic, military, and agricultural traps, we wind up in the end getting *our* tails gnawed off.

How do you reconcile your cherished notions with the un-cherished facts of life? Can the realities of sin and the necessity of grace be realized in such a way that we can still cling to our cherished notions of a peaceful world?

Perhaps that is why we have such a large New Testament. If all we needed were cherished notions then the great God in his infinite wisdom would have simply given us the ethical teachings of Jesus. These could be printed on a six-page brochure. If all we needed were absolute ideals to cherish we could carry a little booklet in our pockets instead of these bulky Bibles. But we have a variety of writings in the New Testament and we have all those letters from Paul to churches.

One of my Furman professors, T. C. Smith,[10] says we owe the richness of the New Testament largely to the fact that so many of the first Christians, like the ones at Corinth, Rome, and Philippi, were such a sorry lot of people. If those cherished notions of Jesus had not run headlong into a cantankerous and evil world, then we wouldn't have much of a New Testament. The New Testament was written in response to, and often in flagrant reaction to what was happening in the churches.

How can the realities of sin be comprehended in such a way that we can still cling to our Christian notions of a peaceful world? The answer is right there in the eighth chapter of the book of Romans. It is part of the issue in a great argument Paul has been spinning about salvation. Salvation is not entirely visible yet, says Paul. It is part of a tremendous project God has been working on. The Jewish people were part of this project. The coming of Christ was part of it. And now our cooperation with the Spirit of God is part of it. And we are moving toward a New Age, an age in which the earth will know a splendor and a peace it has never known. But *we aren't there yet.* We don't see that peace yet. The world is still imperfect. It is not yet the way God intends it to be. When we submit to the Spirit of God, we become God's helpers in an unfinished world. Paul is correct: "Hope that is seen is not hope. For who hopes for what he sees? But if we hope for what we do not see, we wait for it with patience." (Romans 8:24-25)

Christianity tells it like it is — in order to be happy a person has to live in hope for these cherished notions that we cannot yet see. Jesus' teachings focus on the ends of life, what people live for. The Bible says nothing about euthanasia, modern medicine, computers, jet travel, and agricultural economy. But the Bible has much to say about what we are to live *for.* We are to work to improve the ends for which people live as God's helpers in an unfinished world.

And that is where we are falling short. Our generation has been so absorbed in the provision of more *means* by which to live and the creation of more necessary military security that we have failed to tell our children the *ends* for which we are living. Are we living for great ends?

Look at the whole panorama of human history. A little group of disciples surrounded a master teacher in Galilee. Their *means* of living were crude. They walked virtually everywhere they went. Their houses had only one room. The family slept on a high platform and their animals slept on the floor beneath them. The smell must have been awful! By our standards, those stone holes of existence would be called poverty stricken. But think of the ends for which they lived. They upheld some cherished notions in the midst of their evil world. They helped God in the finishing of his world. Yes, they did.

Look at the Greeks, a people small in number. They were primitive in their means. And look at the uncherished facts of their existence. They were surrounded by Egyptians who spent fortunes preserving dead bodies. They encountered the Assyrians who worshipped gods that were half animal. They rubbed shoulders with hoards of people so illiterate they had to carry weapons everywhere they went. But in that environment they helped God toward the finishing of his world. They upheld some cherished notions, drawing no racial, social, or national boundaries. They lived for great ends.[11] They were fired by great hopes. Into that culture one day walked a man named Paul. He looked around and he liked what he saw. These people had never met Jesus, but their cherished notions were on target. Paul said to the people of Athens that he could see they were a religious people. They were living for the same things as Christians were living for. So Paul proceeded to make known to them the God who previously had been unknown. Paul learned from that Greek world. He set out to preach a universal religion in the international language which was Greek. Without those hundreds of years in which the Greek people lived in hope of something they could not see, we would not have a Bible.

We must uphold and communicate to our family and friends the cherished ideals for which we live in our unfinished world. That is our gift to give the world. That is our way to help God finish his creation.

What must we as a nation uphold as we wrestle with the uncherished facts in our violent world?

Our economy? Certainly. But the world has seen great economic empires come and go before. All we need do is look at the empires of Persia, Rome, and Britain to see how feeble that contribution can become. Our system of government? Certainly. But France, Britain, the Aztecs, and the Mayans all had their day of great governments. Our security of defense? Certainly. But all we need do is look at the empires of Gengis Khan, Portugal, Prussia, Persia, Egypt and the Philistines to see how feeble that contribution can become. No, our contribution is to bring to the uncherished facts of our existence, the cherished notions of Jesus Christ to hope in some things we cannot yet fully see — peace, meekness, righteousness, mercy and purity of heart.

No truer words were spoken than those by the great Jeiwsh Pharisee, Gamaliel. In Acts 5, Peter and the apostles have filled Jerusalem with some new notions. And Peter has exclaimed, "we must obey God rather than men." Apparently they were witnesses to something no one else could see. So Gamaliel rather wisely said, "Leave them alone." Then he clicked off in rapid-fire succession a number of people who arose and came to nothing. But he knew that if an undertaking came from God it would not fail and no one would be able to overthrow it. And he was right.

No matter how uncherished have been the facts of existence

and human sin, no power has ever overthrown certain cherished notions and the people who have lived by them.

That is our contribution to God's continued effort to finish his creation. We must live for peace in a world of violence. Such is not only necessary for individual health but is necessary from the perspective of affirming human beings as the ultimate intention in God's creation of existence. A life-style of hope affirms the holiness of God's creation. Such helps to undergird the reconcilation between Christian belief and scientific learning.

11

Humankind: High Hopes On The Creator's Part

An issue very much in the news in recent years is the repair of America's bridges. It seems that many of our country's bridges are in disrepair and need to be upgraded. The issue is a lively one as Congress wrestles with the repair of these numerous spans which connect one bank with another bank in our country.

I think of the need for effective bridges when I think of where we stand each Christmas, wanting to effect a tie between today's world and the world of ancient Bethlehem. The shore of America in our technological society seems far removed from the Bethlehem of Christ's birth. And the bridge of our non-scientific Bible-thumping childhood seems to be in permanent disrepair. Consider the opposites over which we and our children have to traverse.

We stand on the banks of a scientific culture. We live in a world of nuclear reactors, space probes, and computerized technology. Santa Claus leaves under trees various assortments of laser-ray guns, spacemen and spacewomen, and video games. On Christmas day as church bells ring and Luke's account of the birth of Christ is read, many children will be trying to help pac-man gobble blips on a screen and space invaders destroy a planet. And when that lengthy day has passed, they will cuddle up in bed not with a pocket version of the New Testament, but with an extra-terrestial doll. Even we adults wonder at the ever-increasing possibility that one day the heart which beats in our body will have been made in Japan. That's the shore on which we stand, *my friends*. In some ways we probe deeper, fly higher, and understand more than any generation before us.

And we look across an ever-increasing chasm to a distant shore. On that distant shore we see the world of the Bible, with its primitive understandings of science which seem so strangely out of place to our consciousness. We witness people who speak of water being changed to wine; a stick that becomes a serpent, and wisemen, lonely figures against the eternal sand motivated by some impulse they could but dimly understand, journeying day after day, month after month, following a star to a stable. These people believe that somehow the child they found was linked with God. They believe that this child grew up to become a man who preached love and that when he died his spirit slipped out of this earth into something greater than the body which held it.

So here we stand, between two seemingly irreconcilable shores. We see the scriptural accounts of the creation, the exodus, and the birth of Jesus. But we see those accounts from the vantage point of a culture that is instinctively scientific, mistrustful, and cautious.

Some people tell us there is no bridge we can build between our generation and ancient Bethlehem; we must choose one of the two shores and stay there. These people stand in the Biblical accounts, found schools and churches where the Bible is taken literally as a science book, and argue that we should disregard evolution, and the 20th century.

Still others tell us we must stand in the scientific world and throw out the Biblical accounts as mere products of the active human imagination in pre-scientific, superstitious cultures. "The Bible," they say, "is outmoded for our times and can't stand up to the evidence."

So we stand and look at the two apparently distant shores and say, "I want to find out how I got here and who I am before I die." *Can we build a bridge between modern society and ancient Bethlehem that answers the primal cry for understanding in terms that will make sense to our children and ourselves?* Can we reconcile the cherished notion of a Saviour with the realities of modern science?

That seems to me to be a need our faith ought to be able to satisfy if our hope is to be well-founded. If the reasons behind the birth of Jesus as the Son of God cannot stand the tests of scientific discovery and intellectual inquiry, few people, in my opinion, should even believe in God. If God does not make sense in our time, God will not make sense at all. If our hopes are not based in some scientific possibility, they are not hopes. They are *illusions.* We have no less an authority on this than Jesus himself. Jesus said the *truth,* not superstition, would make us free. He had little patience with those who could not discern the presence of God in their own times. "You, hypocrites," he asserted, "you can understand the weather and science ... how is it you do not discern this time?" (Luke 12:56)

Consequently, I believe Jesus demands that I build a bridge for my children and myself between the scientific and the biblical-world-views, in order to bring together ancient Bethlehem and modern America. *This book is nothing more nor nothing less than my bridge.*

Scientists tell us our universe had a birth fifteen or so billion years ago in what they call a "black hole." Before that, there was nothing. How our universe came out of a black hole is a mystery. We think we know that a fireball came out of an exploding black hole 15 billion years ago. When the fireball cooled down, stars and our sun were formed. Finally, the dense nova stars blew up and formed our solar system. It took billions of years and incredible vastness of space. The question is obvious: why did it take so long and why is the universe so large? The only way to answer that is to say that *human life had to be the ultimate purpose of creation.* If 15 billion years ago, human beings were the idea in mind when the black hole exploded, the universe would have to be this old and this large. A younger and smaller universe could not have created human life. The universe would have to be *at least* 9 billion years old. Five billion years would be necessary just to produce DNA and RNA codes. Another four billion years of ever-increasing complex evolution would be necessary to get a man and a woman. The human being is the most complex organism that has appeared so far. Scientific discoveries of the incomprehensible age and vastness of the universe cause us to rejoice. It had to be this old and this large if human life were the purpose for its creation.[12]

Consider also when the fireball began to be our universe, three constants were built into the process. Three items were constant. The speed with which light travels is always 186,000 miles per second. That is a given in our universe. Secondly, the electrical charge of an electron is always constant. Finally, there is a unit called h cross (ℏ) by scientists. An electron as it rotates always jumps by that unit. Its angular momentum *always* jumps by ℏ. Now those three constants blew out of that black hole. Scientists have devised a formula using those three constants (E^2/hc) and have come up with the stable figure *137.06* for our universe. They have played with that figure greatly. Suppose the speed of light was 185,000 feet per second? Suppose the unit of angular momentum was just a little different? If we had 136 or 137.05 or any other figure instead of 137.06, our universe could not have produced human life.

When our universe was created, somebody or something set those constants so human life could eventually be created. You can't explain it any other way. Humanity was the purpose for our universe.

The scientists phrased it this way: "Humankind was created in the image of God. Humankind is more than the fortuitous combination of atoms." C. S. Lewis, in *Christian Reflections,* says it like this:

> *There are no ordinary people. You have never talked to a mere mortal . . . It is immortals whom we joke with, marry, snub, and exploit . . . Next to the Blessed Sacrament itself, your neighbor is the holiest object presented to your senses.*[13]

The one born in ancient Bethlehem told us that the greatest thing in life is to love God with all our being and love our neighbor as we love ourselves. The essential thrust of Jesus' ministry was *the radical concept that the neighbor is holy,* because the human personality is the purpose for creation.

That radical concept, to my mind, is our bridge with ancient Bethlehem.

I once knew a man who stood by his daughter through two difficult marriages and a five-year bout with drugs. Even through some of the worst human conditions I have ever been exposed to, this man kept hanging in there, performing one incredible act of love and kindness after another. When she had attained stability, someone asked him what strength he had drawn on. He said, "I helped give her life and had invested 21 years in her. I just wasn't going to let her kill herself without at least a glimpse of some goodness."

The author of the scenario of cosmic evolution, the one who spent five billion years just producing DNA and RNA codes, the one who set the speed of light, the quantum of angular momentum, and the electrical charge of an electron — *the one who had* ting us to life — was not willing to let the summation of creation destroy itself without at least a glimpse of its holiness. Jesus Christ was born to enable a fallible struggling creation to gain a glimpse of its creator. Even when this creation rejected that glimpse and nailed it to a cross, God in the death event continued to enable the world to have a peek at its holiness.

I am afraid our world has a tendencey to reverse the issue. The issue is not trying to understand the angels, the accounts of miracles, and the scene in ancient Bethlehem in terms that make sense scientifically. The issue is this: we cannot understand science, the age and vastness of the universe, and the three constants of existence without ancient Bethlehem. Without understanding humankind as the intended purpose for creation, our world just doesn't make sense.

What a profound ramification that is for the way we should treat life. It means *a woman is holy.* A woman is more than the sum of her child bearings and miscarriages. She is more than years and years of standing at the sink developing popped veins as the symbol of weary worlds of work. A woman is holy. She is more than the source of a second income or a professional who hammers out a career or a single person living contentedly in singleness. *A woman is holy.*

It means a man is holy. A man is more than a once-young person who has a particular job and whose original physique has waned into flabbiness or grayness. *A man is holy.*

It means a poor person is more than a poor person. A poor person is holy. It means that a diseased and infirmed person is more than one whose best years are spent. *A person is holy.*

From the shepherds, to the lepers, to the rich and haughty, to the demonic, to the fishermen, to the tax collectors, to the publicans, to the thief on the cross, to the technicians, to the nuclear scientists, to the business people, to the homemakers, to the children playing video games, to the children lying in bed with the E. T. dolls, *the message comes cascading over the tumults of time — God is with us.*

The wisest people of the world are not those who have delved *message comes cascading over the tumults of time — God is with us.*

The wisest people of the world are not those who have delved into the great libraries of the world; nor are they those who have sat at the feet of the great teachers. *The wisest people in the world are those who can look to ancient Bethlehem and catch a glimpse of its holiness.* That glimpse cannot only fire our eternal hopes, but when coupled with the crucifixion and resurrection, can enable us to live by faith in a world of chance.

12

Hope In Spite of Chance, Bad Luck and Randomness

In the town where I was raised, North Augusta, South Carolina, there is an intersection in a residential area which I have skillfully avoided for the past 18 years. Even when a trip would be made shorter by going directly through that intersection, I still go around it.

There are two houses at that intersection that I haven't laid eyes on in 18 years. Haven't wanted to really. In one house lived a childhood friend of mine named Ed Arnold. When I was engaged in high school athletics, young Ed was the up and coming superstar in baseball and basketball. At age 16, Ed stood 6' 5" tall and weighed 205 pounds. He was a gentle, lovable, fine Christian fellow. Everyone loved Ed. Then, Ed developed cancer. Within six months he was dead. At the age of 17, he still was 6' 5" tall but he weighed exactly 68 pounds when he turned over and died.

In the other house, directly across from Ed Arnold, lived Jane Eddins. Jane and I were the best of friends in high school. There were few people as pretty, kind, and fun-to-be-with as Jane Eddins. We went to ball games together, always saved at least a page for each other to write on in our high school annuals, and even went together on a trip to the Rocky Mountains, over 1500 miles away. One night she and her brother were returning to our town from the University of South Carolina. A car driven by a person under the influence of alcohol careened out of control, smashed into the Eddins' car and decapitated Jane. She, like Ed, was 17 years old when she was buried.

So I avoid that intersection in my old hometown. It's more than a place where two residential roads intersect. *It's the place where my belief in a kind, loving God to whom I pray and in whom I believe, intersects with the randomness and suffering in the world which prompts me to question even the existence of a caring God.*

Now I suggest that all of us have such an intersection in our lives. Some of us are able to avoid it for long periods, but that still doesn't make it go away. Others among us have to live very close to that intersection all of our days because of its ever-present claim on our lives through events in our own families. Harold Kushner is perhaps correct: There is only one question which really matters: why do bad things happen to good people?"[14]

Can we really believe the world is good and that God is a kind and loving God? The world is certainly not a neat and just place. Any hope we possess must be grounded in a just God.

I do not intend to give a pat answer to the problem of suffering. Far from it. But I firmly believe we can strengthen our faith in order to live *with* the sufferings we must all face.

To be certain, there is a randomness in the universe. We do live in a world of chance. Although we are born with biologically inherited characteristics, no moral intelligence decided for us which of the millions of sperm would fertilize a waiting egg. We were born as we are, by chance. There are accidents, weather conditions, and failures that are also apparently randomly determined. And God appears to take a hands-off approach to this randomness. On the other hand, life surely must be more than a gigantic game of Russian roulette. If God is personally interested in what happens in the world and loves us as he says he does, then there ought to be some explanation for the suffering we face. If God is powerful and good, it did not do Ed Arnold and Jane Eddins any good. Did it? Did it do their friends any good to hope for their well-being?

The Old Testament presents us with a clear example of the question about good and evil in the form of a man named Job. Here was a godly man who suffered calamity after calamity. He lost his property, his health, his children, and the love of his wife. Yet people not as good as Job were prospering. It really wasn't fair. Job didn't deserve his fate. So in utter defiance he finally asked of God the ancient question: "Why me?"

In typical fashion, some counsellors came to Job and offered him five ridiculous answers. First, they said the world makes sense so there must be some reason for your suffering. Job didn't buy that. The world doesn't make sense and there isn't any *reason* for it. Then Job was told that life is tough and not to be surprised when things go wrong. Fortunately, Job didn't buy that either. Life is tougher for some folks than it is for others. Next, they told Job to simply "be patient." What ridiculous advice. So finally they gave Job the age old cop-out for God, "suffering is good for you." Job didn't buy that either. *Suffering is not good. It is bad.*

Finally, there came a whirlwind and out of that terrible windstorm God answers Job with these words: "What do you know about how to run a world?" God's response is to live with the mystery. There are mysteries that will always remain. But God responds that his love and concern operate in this world of change. God cares for a sparrow and even keeps track of the gestation period of the mountain goat.[15]

My God! How do we interpret that response? First of all, it means that God allows pain and mystery in the world but does not deliberately inflict it. God has created a free universe with morally free creatures. *God can allow something to happen that God doesn't will to happen.* Not everything that happens is God's will. *God has set limits on God.* God will not intervene to take away our freedom, even the freedom to hurt ourselves and others. We have a wrought iron fire poker by the fireplace in our den. I could use it to hit someone on the head. I could kill someone with it even if they are a morally better person than I am. God could have created a world so that our iron poker would become as soft as bread when I unjustly used it as a weapon. But that would leave me with no responsibility to use it properly. In like manner, cancer will eat up an Ed Arnold even if he is a better person than someone who is free from cancer. And an out of control automobile will kill indiscriminately. Unlike other animals we humans have the capacity to understand both the indiscriminate nature of God's creation and our own eventual death. It's quite a burden for humans to carry.

Perhaps you have read or seen the television account of Colleen McCullough's novel, *The Thornbirds.* It chronicles the life of a family in the harsh "outback" lands of Australia. As I peeped in on that family from my vantage point as a reader, I had an overwhelming urge to play God. I encountered a little girl whose personality was forever scarred by an elementary school teacher. She was treated with less dignity, because of her poverty, than the children of people who rode to school in big cars and donated buildings and organs to the town church. I wished I could have reached down into the book, picked the little girl up and placed her in another school with another teacher, but I could not.

I encountered a son fighting with his father. He left home in helpless anger. He fell in with the wrong people who turned his life into violence and landed him in prison. i wished I could have reached into the book and placed him with different friends. But I could not.

I could not go into the lives of these people and manipulate them at will if the chief intent in their creation was their freedom to make their own history. They must be free to live long or short lives, suffer innocently or deservedly and choose their own responses to living in a world of chance and freedom. That is God's dilemma in relating to us humans.

If you were God, how would *you* handle life? Imagine, if you were a loving and caring God, what would you do, if the chief intent in our creation was to give us the freedom to make our own history?

I, frankly, can imagine only five things a loving God could possibly do to intervene in our process of life. If I were God, first of all I would have to intervene once and for all for everyone, born and unborn. I could not respond to three or four billion human requests a day. What one human would want would negate what another human would want. The whole system of freedom of choice would go down the drain. It would have to be a one-time, inclusive shot, if I intervened. Secondly, this reconciliation with a suffering world would have to deal with more than one chapter of the human existence. If I loved humans I would have to cover more than just their years on earth because all humans aren't given the same number of years to live on earth. It would have to be an alpha and omega intervention. Thirdly, if I really cared for these humans, I would have to intervene in such a way as to share their suffering. Fourthly, this once-and-for-all, alpha-and-omega, shared-suffering intervention would have to be done in such a way that they could help one another bear the burdens of suffering. And finally, I would have to leave behind something that would enable those humans always to have access to personal communication with me, to constantly remind them that I know their name and will remember them forever.

Now, that, in my opinion, is what a loving God would do to redeem the tragedies of this world from senselessness. Apparently that's what humankind came to see over a 4,000 year period. The Old Testament raised those questions. The Old Testament wanted answers to the unfair, unjust, God-awful tragedies that occur in human existence. It's full of curses against God. The Psalms hoped for a new sovereign who might bring in a new reform movement to champion the poor, weak, and oppressed. But the hope was unfinished. No God showed up to do that. The first Isaiah hoped God, if God was good, would at least cause a representative to be born on earth. Maybe a young woman could give birth to an ideal king who would be a wonderful counselor, a mighty God, a prince of peace. But it did not happen. Then, Jeremiah, two centuries later, looked out on his people shut up like birds in a cage with Babylonia ready to pounce and break what they understood to be a covenant with God. So Jeremiah cursed God and said if God was really good there would be a new covenant not on tablets of stone but on the eternal hearts of people, a covenant not just for one race but for all people. But it never happened, In this world of chance, Nebuchadnezzer crushed Jeremiah and put his people in exile for 500 years.

Then a second Isaiah wrote a message from that horrible exile: "Why do we suffer? If God is so great, so all-loving, let's hope he'll do the miraculous and send us a suffering servant to identify with our pain. Wouldn't a really good God comfort his people and suffer alongside of them?" But, friends, it just did not happen. Another writer from exile, the author of the book of Job, just came out and said it: "Why do the innocent suffer if God is so good?" Why do we have such a disease ridden, non-loving, unjust, calamitous, slop-bin existence if God is so good?" Why, indeed, is there not a once and for all, all inclusive, forever-intervention by a God who is good and will know our suffering to the extent something can be left behind to account for all the tragedies of random existence? Like a tidal wave the rush of human history shouted its bewildered cry. Hope after hope seemed to come to naught.

If the life of the human race from its creation to the present could be captured on motion picture film, *all the frames in that film combined would not add up in importance to the one where this Jesus of Nazareth cries, "It is finished," and pitches his head forward in the death on the cross.* That crucifixion took nearly nine hours. It was a slow death, the muscles degenerating into knobs of agony. There was nothing civilized about it. Paul tells us "God was in Christ reconciling the world . . . "(2 Corinthians 5:19). Think of it. God — *hanging like a slab of meat on some spikes.* Most of the faithful never showed up. Those who came were for the most part ignorant hecklers who spat and cursed. God in Christ looked down on a scene of madness, cried, "It is finished," and slumped over into eternity. But God stuck to the rules when the Son cried out. God didn't unpin him. God did not play games with Pilate's freedom of choice, or negate the power of the Pharisees. It is indeed a random existence, a world of chance. *But it was finished!*

God knows our pain and becomes completely approachable even as we walk through the valley of the shadow of death. God sent us the strength to cope with existence. Existence is still something we should get angry at. At times it is rotten, unfair, and undeserved. *But it is finished!*

God always has the *last word* in human affairs. The apostle Paul records these words from God when he sought help for his thorn in the flesh: "My grace is sufficient for you, for my power is made perfect in weakness."

I have seen some incredible tragedies redeemed from senselessness through the love and power of God. It is finished and there is a grace sufficient for our living in a sometime rotten, unfair, and untimely world of chance.

It was finished long before you and I were born. And it is finished for others who will be born long after our death.

I think the next time I go back to my hometown I'll ride throught the intersection again. Maybe I'll even get out of the car and walk around. When the issue is decided and there is a grace that penetrates the randomness of human existence, a person can see beyond the shadow of the present. *You can live by faith in a world of chance.*

Once one encounters the possibilities of a life of hopeful living, the possibilities are powerful beyond belief. In spite of our modern dilemmas, one can lift the psychological ceiling on one's hope in order to embrace the unseen, reconcile cherished notions of peace with uncherished facts about violence, embrace scientific inquiry and live by faith in a world of chance. Jesus certainly

tainly thought it possible. In fact, such hopeful living is our only hope. We can actually serve as lights of kindness in a rough world. Our life-styles can reflect, and indeed must reflect, those internal characteristics which evidence the hope in Christ which sustains us.

Part Three

The Life-Styles Of Hope

13

Cause For Hope: Kindness In A Tough World

My sister was an avid reader of movie star gossip magazines. Near the back of those magazines were sections advertising pen pals. For some unexplained reason the idea of having a pen pal stuck in my consciousness. So I tore that section out of one of the magazines.

Being a red-blooded male teenager at the time, I naturally selected the name of a female teenager as my designated pen pal. The girl lived in Germany and I wrote her a long, glowing letter describing , with some embellishment, my hometown and the various activities in my life. She returned an equally descriptive letter and our correspondence was off to a successful start.

For almost three years we faithfully exchanged letters. I delighted in telling my friends about the gorgeous German girl I was acquainted with. And each time I sat in the den reading those exciting letters written in broken English from Offenbach, Germany, I thought of the beautiful girl with the shapely figure who had composed them. Those letters met many of my teenage needs.

Finally, the inevitable happened. I wrote my German friend that it might be nice if we exchanged pictures. She agreed. So, on a cold, windy winter day I went over to a shopping mall in Augusta, Georgia, and got inside a booth where you get three pictures made for a quarter. I smiled a cheesecake smile for three quick flashes. Dutifully and expectantly I mailed the pictures to Germany. Our letters crossed in the mail and an envelope arrived for me only a few days later. I eagerly tore it open and removed the contents.

After that day I never wrote another letter to a pen pal. My expectations had far exceeded reality. And, *strangely enough,* the girl in Germany never wrote me again, either!

Unfortunately, at that time in life *I did not possess the, perspective needed to see* traits of personhood like kindness, humility, and truth. *All my emotional self-indulgence could see was the superficial.*

Now, my story is the story of much of the cynicism in the world. The Bible is basically a chronicle of the gaps that have persisted in the expectations we humans have laid on God and the way God has actually worked in reality.

Such was the case with those who eagerly looked for a messiah. Conditions in that society were most difficult for the Jewish people. They longed for a God who would vindicate them. Oppressed and hurt as they were, they conceived images of one who would breathe fire and overturn the stratified social system. Those on the bottom in life wanted to be on the top. We can discern this thinking in the book of Revelation and other apocalyptic books. The Saviour is imagined as one who would separate the sheep from the goats. The earth would be obliterated and the Jewish people would rise from their graves and take pleasure killing those who had persecuted them.

John the Baptist felt this way. John came preaching repentance and baptising people in the River Jordan. Many Pharisees and Sadducees came to be baptized. But John had an emotional image of what the Messiah would look like. He stopped his work and screamed, "You brood of vipers! Who warned you to flee from the wrath to come?"

John fully expected this messiah to come full of anger and hate. "His winnowing fork is in his hand," said John. "He will burn you and baptize with the Holy Spirit and he will singe you with fire."

Scripture records that John was thrown completely off track when his expectation clashed with the reality of Jesus. Jesus was baptized and the Spirit of God descended like a dove. A dove! The symbol of peace and calmness clashed with John's expectations of wrath and fire. What kind of prophet was this? A dove! Prophets are supposed to be cynical, angry folk who stand the world on its ear. It was like expecting Burt Reynolds and getting Truman Capote. Kindness! My God, what can we do with kindness!

The reality of Jesus differed so much from some people's hopes for a successful messiah that they reacted the way I did when I saw my pen pal's picture. No more! Never again! Why doesn't God do something to change the mess of the world? Why doesn't God show his real face?

The raucous noises fill the public places in our time. We're doomed. Nuclear war threatens. The social conditions of the planet are monstrous. Where is the transforming God with world-wide consequence? Why doesn't God show his face or at least send us a prophet? In the face of racial discrimination, economic avarice, and dedication of science to destructive purposes, we want a God with a winnowing fork in his hand, and a fire to boot! Clean it up!

It probably doesn't dawn on us that God's prophets have always been as kind as they have been flashy and abrasive. More than a few first-century citizens likened Jesus to Jeremiah and Elijah. Something about the carpenter's son caused them to identify him with those men of old. *I believe it was the flaming light of kindness which tied those three together.* That light of kindness which threw John the Baptist off guard is something we need to see in a tough world.

Examine clearly the story of Elijah. He lived in a time of political tyranny. It was a tough world. The king of Israel was a bad seed named Ahab. Ahab was corrupt to the core but his wife, Jezebel, was really something else. She was Madylyn Murray O'Hare, Racquel Welch, and Bonnie Parker rolled into one. Elijah appeared on the scene as God's representative. He boldly announced that God was going to unseat *both* of them. To say the least, the political establishment was furious. To add insult to their injury, Elijah announced that there would be a drought — no rain for three years. Such a dire forecast caused Elijah to be run out of the country. The only safe place he could find was in the household of a widow in a little non-Israelite village. While he was there a terrible crisis developed. The widow's son became ill to the point of death. Naturally she blamed it on Elijah.

And, Elijah, one of the great debaters of all times — so eloquent he could preach the bark off a pine tree — became quiet! He went to the perishing boy and took him to an upper room. There he apparently practiced mouth to mouth resuscitation and cried to God to let life return to the boy. God heard his prayer.

What about that? In the midst of a tough world, in the middle of a revolution, this progressive, abrasive man, stopped to be kind. This light of kindness caught the woman off guard: it was not what she expected from God. For the very first time she saw Elijah as a man of God.

Jesus left us that legacy: read the Sermon on the Mount. It is not the type of swashbuckling posture you look for to turn the world on its ear. He speaks of salt, leaven in a loaf, and a light set on a hill. These are not the anticipated images of hope, are they?

So crucial was Jesus' insistence on the power of kindness that he paralleled Elijah. He took his disciples, these individuals ready to vindicate God at the drop of a hat, to an upper room to breathe into them as Elijah had done centuries before. But whereas Elijah faced a boy who was physically sick, Jesus faced people who were *mentally* perishing in their tough world. Their hope had turned to despair; their expectations had gone sour, their security had turned to disillusionment; their images clashed with reality. Their hope had vanished. There in the upper room Jesus breathed into their bodies the only thing that would last — the peace that passes all understanding — *a posture of kindness in a tough world. Those little lights grew into the most momentous forces for good our world has ever seen.* What turned out in the end to be of world-transforming consequence began so quietly, so unostentatiously, that contemporaries well nigh missed it: *little lights of kindness in a tough world.*

All saving ideas are born small, like mustard seed. That's difficult for us to see — the show under the big tent doesn't matter most nor last the longest.

The greatest need in our time is for us to regain a sense of being individually needed and individually called for. The greatness of a whole nation is inextricably bound up with its individuals. We must say, "this means *me*. It means me and *my* life, *my* best self, *my* highest ideals, if something magnificent is tgo be realized in my generation." This troubled time is not the end of humankind's road. If you can feel the music of God in your soul, turn on your light of kindness. *It's amazing what little lights of kindness can accomplish in a tough world.*

It is a temptation to believe that we are made great by our power yet ruined by our humility. In fact, even our handicaps can be overcome, lived with and conscripted in God's service to build a hopeful world. We cannot totally avoid our handicaps. All of us have minuses somewhere. The key is whether or not our hopes will enable us to turn our minuses into pluses.

14

The Hopeful Equation:
Turning A Minus Into A Plus

All our seas are not smooth ones. The apostle Paul recognized this. As a wise, old seasoned veteran of life's battles, Paul wrote a letter to a young man named Timothy. This great man of God, who wrote over one-third of our New Testament, described life in these terms: "It is a fight, and I have fought a good one. It is a race, apparently a hard race, to run and still keep your faith. But I have finished that difficult race and still kept my faith. Hence there is a crown of righteousness waiting on me."

The assumption is one can take whatever minuses one encounters along the way of life, shoulder these, and even carry them right to the very end to a crown of righteousness. Jesus the Christ lived that example of turning minuses into pluses. In the Old Testament when Job was confronted with all manner of calamities and handicaps, his wife told him the best thing to do was to "curse God and die." In his wife's perspective, he was ruined by all these minuses he could do nothing about. But Jesus felt differently. "If you want to come after me," he said, "you must deny yourself, take up that cross and follow me."

The entire New Testament seems to be a chronicle of the lives of people who have emptied themselves before God and with God as the center of their lives, turned their minuses into pluses. I call this to our attention because we live in a world that has tended to forget that power available to it.

Sometimes we routinely move through our world of habit, taking life's little miracles for granted. No wonder we feel bored and brittle, thin and dry, when we step out on that road to run the race and fight the fight. There is a power with sparkle and resonance that can be a tremendous ally to us. And I want simply to remind us of that fact, so that having eyes we may see, and having ears we may hear.

Consider this. On even the most routine morning of a harried homemaker in High Point, N.C., where I live, virtually everything she touches is a living example of a minus having been turned into a plus. For example, she wakes up and turns on a light bulb that was perfected by a deaf man. Then she moves into the kitchen and turns on the radio to listen to the news, or a local personality, or some form of music. Never does it dawn on her that the radio was invented by a hunchback. If she listens to contemporary music, it probably doesn't register that three of the six most popular artists in the country providing the music are blind. Perhaps next she dresses and goes in her automobile to the Fresh Market, a store where she shops for groceries while enjoying a Beethoven symphony written by a classical composer who was stone deaf. Finally, with the shopping done, she rushes to pick up the children at school or to meet their bus. Certainly it never dawns on her that the greatest achievement in education was made by a woman born unable to see, unable to hear and unable to speak.

Her story is our story. Indeed, life is a stormy sea at times; a rough road; a personhood littered with apparent minuses. And we wonder if religion really makes any difference as we walk that walk.

But our God is a mighty God. And the creative impulse is a mighty impulse. Her story is also our story in that *virtually everything we touch was invented and sustained by someone who turned a minus into a plus.* How do we tap into that remarkable force in life? What kind of prayers do we pray to bring about that incredible conversion in our own moments of frailty? What tangible difference does religion really make in turning a minus into a plus?

I think a very good clue to the magnitude of God's power is in the fortieth chapter of Isaiah:

> but they who wait for the Lord
>   shall renew their strength,
> They shall mount up with wings like
>   eagles,

They shall run and not be weary,
They shall walk and not faint.

> (Isaiah 40:31 RSV)

Look at the forms of help from God in the passage. John Claypool[16] has noted that some people feel Isaiahs passage is all turned around and the highest form of God's help ought to be the soaring of ecstasy. They say it should build up this way, "first you walk, then you run, and finally you mount up with wings as an eagle." That is how you turn a minus into a plus — you walk, run and then soar. But the writer of this passage knew God and he knew life. He set down the promises as he did in perfect ascending order, for the greatest gift is reserved for the most difficult problem, that of keeping on when life has slowed you to a walk, when it seems that in spite of everything you're better off just caving in to the negatives.

God's help is described in three forms. There is the promise that God's help can take the form of ecstasy, enabling us to mount up and soar like eagles. Many times we have felt such joy and celebration in our religious experience. Jesus felt that when he was baptized and the dove descended upon him. He felt it at the moment when he rode the donkey into Jerusalem as the crowds shouted Hosanna to the Son of David. Paul felt it when the scales fell from his eyes and once again when he set foot on European soil. And the women felt it when they gazed into the empty tomb. Sometimes God turns minuses into pluses in a dramatic fashion.

But you and I know that those occasions are very rare, if at all. If divine possibilities were limited to the quick-fix method, you and I would experience little basis for hope. Fortunately, scripture points to more divine possibilities than the quick-fix. God is not solely the one who comes in with a ballpoint pen and alters the transcript of your life by putting a quick vertical mark through the minus so that it looks like a plus to all concerned. Sometimes he does — but not always.

Isaiah describes a second way God helps us turn minuses into pluses: "They shall run and not be weary." God gives us strength for activism. God gives us the inspiration to act, to reach out and do a task or solve a problem. We can witness the indefatigable spirit of Jesus as he healed, touched, and spoke to countless thousands of people. All of us have prayed to God and found the motivation and power to get busy with projects. I know I certainly have. But again, this is not the only way we experience God's help. Thank goodness. You see, more often than not, there are times when there is really little, of anything, one can do. There are some problems, some deficiencies, some minuses that cannot be attacked by force or energy. Sometimes there is no room to run and not be weary.

But fortunately there is another way in which God can help us turn a minus into a plus. "They shall walk and not faint." Now, if we're seeking the spectacular, that may not sound like much. Who wants to walk, to barely creep along inch by inch, barely above the threshold of existing, not fainting? That does not sound like much of a religious experience does it? But, friends, most of our decisions in life are made when there is no occasion to soar and no place to run, and all you can do is trudge along, and hear that a help is available. When there is a power enabling us to walk and not faint, that is indeed good news. It speaks to the greatest difficulty: being able to endure, to be patient and not to give way to heading in another direction.[17] From the flight to Egypt as a baby, to his night in Gethsemane, to his trial before Herod, to his march with the cross to his crucifixion, the greatest power available to Jesus was the power to hang in there, to walk and not faint, to cling to his situation and not abandon his task.

John Mortimer was an English barrister.[18] He became a great writer. His autobiography possessed a catching title. He called it *Clinging to the Wreckage*. He says it came to him one day when he was lunching with a yachtsman. He asked the yachtsman if sailing the ocean was dangerous. The man replied it was not if you never learn to swim. He explained: "When you're in a spot of trouble, if you can swim you try to strike out for the shore. You invariably drown. As I can't swim, I cling to the wreckage and they send a helicopter out for me. That's my tip, if you ever find yourself in trouble, cling to the wreckage."

That may be one of the most crucial lessons in life: the ability to learn how to start with what you have and build from that, instead of abandoning what you have and swimming for the seductive but distant shores. Every existence has its small share of special feelings, and bonding moments. Sometimes they seem very remote. But they form a more solid launching pad for the future than the non-experiences of the already established silver platter. If you've never learned to "walk and not faint," you have never developed inventiveness and leadership. A sailor who has never sailed in rough seas is never a true sailor.

A few years ago, I had a series of unique opportunities. In one six-month span I spent an evening with the new secretary of state of Belgium, spent eight days with the United States Permanent Ambassador to NATO in the embassy residence in Brussels, ate supper with Admiral Falls, Supreme Commander of all NATO armed forces, and entertained the Cultural Minister of the People's Republic of China during his first trip to the United States. To each of these knowledgeable people I posed a question: "What do you perceive to be the most prevalent weakness in this generation of Americans?"

To my surprise, each person in various forms pointed to the same thing. The perceived weakness is an inability to create a spirit of leadership and inventiveness among our youth. They see our current generation moving through revolving doors of silver platters, looking for one established experience after another. That pioneer spirit, of making a plus out of a minus, holding to the fight, running the race in faith, seems to have given way to impulsive grabbing of the already established.

Fear of failure is a great enemy to a hopeful life-style. We are pioneers for The Kingdom, not recipients of the silver platter. We must envision the harvest of life and develop our self-esteem as God's children. We must cultivate the ability to call on the God who enables us to stand alone and lead, to walk and not faint, regardless of the circumstances. We must embrace the hope we find in our actual selves and circumstances. Such should form the basis for our self-esteem.

15

Hope for Everyone: the Gift of Self-Esteem

Can you *remember* the first time your *actual* self, with your abilities and circumstances, did not measure up to your ideal picture of yourself? I can. When I was a child the church to which my family belonged held a Christmas pageant every year. All the choirs sang and certain members of the oldest children's choir provided a live nativity scene. The highlight of the year for those children in the choir came when they voted on who would play Mary and Joseph. Anyone could play the wisemen. And the director had to beg children to play the shepherds. But Mary and Joseph, now they were the prizes. Since I held the dubious distinction of most hyperactive choir member and grandest fraternizer, I assumed the voting to be a mere formality. Obviously I would play Joseph and my self-perceived girlfriend, Susan, would play Mary. I even had in mind which bathrobe I would wear and which towel I would drape over my head.

But a strange thing happened. Susan was indeed elected to play Mary. But after a run-off, a new boy in town was elected to play Joseph. It was the first time I *remember* having experienced a loss of self-esteem. I felt as if something deep inside of me had died. And in a way it had.

Obviously that was not the last election I ever lost. And it certainly was not the last time I lost my self-esteem. You see, self-esteem is the meshing of our actual selves with our desired selves. *When our actual self does not measure up to our ideal picture of ourself, then we have a hard time accepting ourselves as we really are.* Our actual self is then perceived as less worthy than our imagined self. How do we handle ourselves when we find an impassable chasm between our actual self and our desired self?

It's a tough question because all of us face the gulf between actual and desired self or between actual circumstances and behavior and imagined circumstances and behavior.

Homemakers constantly face the tension between actual self and imagined self as they raise children and lose themselves in preparing meal after meal and doing thousands of washloads of clothes. The actual behavior of a child can conflict with our imaged behavior of a child. And a person in business stitching time and life together in the performance of tasks, faces conditions ripe for touching off the civil war between actual self and desired self. And the war within us is not always an obvious one. Sometimes it becomes buried deep inside our psyche where it gnaws away at our personality for a lifetime. We become people of despair.

Think with me for a moment. *How do you develop love for a child?* When the child is in the mother's womb, the parents engage in grandiose expectations. Every child is, to a degree, expected to be something that it cannot possibly be. Unconsciously we expect our children to be beautiful, healthy, talented, well-mannered, loving, intelligent, and athletic. Is not love the giving up of the unrealistic expectations which cannot possibly be accomplished by the child in favor of constant encouragement and affirmation of the child's actual self? It's the difference between loving an actual person and loving a projection of an ideal. The true test of life is a person's ability to change his projected picture of himself enough to be able to accept himself and go on and make a creditable and serviceable use of the self he/she really has. To make the choice between healthy ambitions and unrealistic demands for perfection.

Jesus the Christ encouraged us to have self-esteem. "Love your neighbor as you love yourself," were his words. Not loving your real self or being out of touch with yourself can make you sick. Worth comes from within a person, not from the outside.

Sometimes something drastic happens to bring us back to our actual selves. An accident. An illness. The loss of a job. A divorce. A failure in business or school. An insight gained through prayer or religious experience. A sense of desperation like that felt by the prodigal son when he finally "came to himself" and decided to go home. *In a sense, Jesus' whole ministry was an invitation to people to get in touch with their truest selves again.* When he said we must become like little children to enter the kingdom, he asserted that we must get beyond the imagined complications and paraphernalia of life to the job and worth of our actual selves.

Perhaps Jesus' most poignant message on self-esteem is to be found in the parable of the sower. The parable was spoken to Jesus' disciples. These men were having a horrible battle between their actual life with Jesus and their imagined life with Jesus. The Galilean campaign was not going well. Their hope was flickering dim. They left their jobs and families in a sense of euphoria and wild-eyed idealism to follow the new king. But the Pharisees resisted the authority of Jesus. He and his disciples became unacceptable in the synagogues and often met hostility. The disciples were discourage by the ups and downs. Some of the Galilean crowds were very small. Much of their work had come to nothing. They wondered if their effort had not been wasted. They had scattered widely like the farmer with the seed and their actual situation had fizzled in comparison with their imagined harvest.

Jesus' parable faces failure head-on. There is much in life that has no depth. The wind can blow it away. And sometimes you can throw out your truth and expectations on open ground and gossip or inconvenience can come and eat them up like a bird. And sometimes who you are and what you have to offer in life can get thrown among the rocks. The rocks of cynicism can crush most anything. And sometimes the thorns and the seeds wind up in a place vieing for the same nourishments.

All that is true. But *the disciples had become so mesmerized by the apparent failures they could see in their desired selves that they lost sight of the colossal harvest beyond expectation, there for the taking if they would but use their actual selves.*

It is as if Jesus were saying, "The key to success is an initial self-acceptance, as though to say, I, Matthew; or I, Mark; or I, Luke, hereby accept this life with its inherited handicaps and endowments and with the elements in my environment I cannot alter or control, and so accepting myself, I will see what I can do with this *actual* Matthew, Mark or Luke in this *actual* situation." Do this, said Jesus, and the harvest will be a hundred fold in your life and in God's work. There is no get rich quick scheme. Focus on the good ground and the harvest will far exceed that which is lost on the rocks and thorns and barren ground.

What a marvelous parable. *If you cannot envision the harvest in your actual situation you can't find it anywhere.* If there is no hope to be found in *your* circumstances, there is no hope.

You know, Jesus also left that parable for the church. Churches possess self-esteem. Churches always have to encounter the tension between what they are and what they want to be. Sometimes the disproportion between actual and imagined ideal is great. This is especially true in an era of mass communications and increased mobility. Now everyone knows what other people have and what they do not have. There is more capacity to focus on the ideal situation and become so mesmerized by the shortfall of the actual than ever before. One year, 1976, I participated in quite a transition (revelation). I left a position as Senior Minister (only minister of a church of 416 members to go to be the Senior Minister of a church with 2,600 members. Strangely enough, the church of 400 members in many ways lamented the fact that it wasn't like the church of 2,600. But the church of 2,600 members was desperately trying to acquire some of the imagined traits like intimacy and fellowship of a 400 member church. For example, the large church felt it needed more intimacy to reap a harvest. So it secured a professional designer and a television communications person to work on improving its "image" as a "family church." Not enough people knew one another. Two of the great things our "family" decided to do were to switch to homemade loaves of bread for communion and have people tear off pieces like they do in a smaller church and then to join hands and sing "Blest Be the Tie." *Do you know how long it takes 900 people to pass around and tear off pieces of bread from loaves?* Thirty-seven minutes! I don't know how long it takes to circle 900 people for "Blest Be the Tie" because that got scratched on the spot.

Now the church of 400 decided we would become more professional in orientation and outreach. We wanted to improve our self-esteem because we were small and always had to look up to the big programs of other churches. We collected professionally printed bulletins and newsletters from larger churches. Fearing we were missing out on something, we hired a professional designer to construct a printed format for us. Then, we reasoned that we would mail these bulletins on a weekly basis to the membership. As part of the process we discovered that you must mail a minimum of 200 pieces under a bulk rate permit. Unfortunately we only had 150 families. So for two years we mailed out 200 bulletins. Some people received one at work and another at their home address. Our English setter, Candy, received one. A pharmacist's collie, Laddie, received one. And the city attorney's cocker spaniel, Buster, always got one. Finally, we decided that in the time it took us each week to be like a big church and mail a bulletin to 165 member units plus eleven dogs, two cats, and nine infants, we could visit seven new families a week in their homes. So we ceased. When we accepted ourselves with our inherited handicaps and endowments, and decided to see what we could do with our *actual* selves, we multiplied in membership a hundredfold.

That's life, my friends. It is true for individuals as it is for institutions. *God made you. If you do not accept yourself, how can you ever accept the God who created you?* When we get in touch with ourselves at the deepest level, we find out that we are sons and daughters of God. We must never get carried away from our origins, our actual selves. The Son of God died for each one of us. His blood was shed, that you and I might know how important we are to God. That is the basis of our self-esteem. No earthly king ever inherited more than you men have inherited. No earthly queen has ever had more royal blood than you women possess.

Jesus wants us to get in touch with ourselves. I do not know all your inherited endowments. But you have them. I do not know what your inherited handicaps are. But you have them. Nor do I know the elements in your environment that you cannot control. But I think I can promise you this: *if you will accept and turn over to God and his church that actual self you are now, right now, not what you think you might be or what you think you ought to be or what you think you used to be, your life will be used to multiply blessings a hundredfold.* Your hope lies not in changing your circumstances but in changing your perception. Hope placed in changing circumstances can become misplaced hope. This is especially true relative to hope for material success.

16

The Kind of Wealth Worth Hoping For

A few years ago I was part of a five-person team assigned to write a proposal for the establishment of a psychiatric hospital. But none of us had ever been hospitalized or institutionalized for a major character disorder. So the United States Department of Education provided us with the opportunity. They found a psychiatric complex in South Carolina that was located across the street from a Ramada Inn. They worked out an arrangement to pay our businesses one week's salary. We were then required to check into the psychiatric unit and the motel. From six a.m. until twelve midnight every day for an entire week we would go through the program with the patients. But at midnight they would let the five of us through the front door to walk over to the Ramada Inn to spend the night. We would go to individual and group sessions but would be there to observe and learn. We would not speak when patients were receiving individual therapy. Other than that, we were full-fledged members of the week's life together. There we were: a colonel in the Army; a hospital administrator; the dean of a school of nursing; a physician; and a Baptist preacher — stuck with that arrangement for a week.

The first impression I received was that no one in the place looked like a problem-plagued individual. In fact, some of the patients appeared to be more solid in terms of background than we were, especially a man named James.

James became my friend. He wore expensive clothes and was most articulate. He had experienced a phenomenal rise in his vocation and in his finances. At age 25 he was a high school principal; when he reached 30 he was a full professor in a large university; at age 34 he became a dean in that same university. Then he dabbled in real estate. He had the "Midas Touch." Everything he bought into turned a large profit. Now, at the age of 38, he apparently was a sick man in spite of his attainments.

Well, I worked it out to attend James' sessions. I did not want to go with someone who was really sick, I reasoned. I might begin to identify with the sickness. And, since James didn't have much wrong with him, that I could ascertain, it would be an easy assignment. Besides, I might even get James to give me some financial advice!

The sessions began. The therapist asked some very pointed questions: "Why do you feel that your wife married you?"

James replied, "Because she loved me!"

"Well, why did she love you? What qualities do you believe attracted her to you?"

James confidently replied, "Because I was bright and aggressive and it appeared that I was a person who would be a success in life. I was definitely on the way up."

The therapist shifted his line of questioning. "Do your children and neighbors like you?"

"Yes, I think so."

With complete candor the therapist retorted, "Why?"

James nervously shifted his feet. "Well, I have a nice home. I provide my family with almost everything the neighbors have. I am respected by the people who associate with me in the various clubs I belong to. I always capably carry out every function I undertake. Oh, yes, occasionally I take the family on an expensive trip."

The therapist pressed his inquiry. "I know other people value your job and position and the things that you provide. But do they like you in and of yourself? Are you happy with yourself? Do you have any feelings of being loved simply for yourself and not the things your skills have generated?" At that point James' confident manner crumbled. His voice wavered, and finally he became silent. His acceptance of reality was about to begin. You see, James' character disorder was the fact that all his feelings of happiness and worth were derived from what he could produce instead of what he was as a human being. His inner worthiness was bound up in external criteria.

The basic cause of much human suffering is the conflict between inner and external values. Jesus thought so, too. The parables of Jesus concerning riches are not about money. They are about people suffering character disorders brought about by their status in life. Jesus never said that wealth is inherently vicious or poverty inherently virtuous. Jesus did not condemn wealth. His first followers were not from homes of poverty but from homes of comfort. Zaccheus and Matthew knew a lot about high finance. The well-to-do centurion who was so wealthy he built a synogogue for the town in which his soldiers were stationed found favor in Jesus' eyes. Jesus ate with the rich more than the poor. The home where he loved to stay and had the most fun, in Bethany with Lazarus, Mary and Martha, was a home of substance. Even the robe Jesus wore was valuable enough for the soldiers to gamble for it at the foot of the cross.

Yet, *almost half the sayings of our Lord concern the right use of riches. Why?*

In the Old Testament God is depicted as rewarding righteous people with earthly riches. If God liked you, he gave you abundant crops, growing herds, and fruitful fields. The great people of the Old Testament like David, Moses, Joseph, Jacob, and Abraham were men of incredible earthly wealth. But in the New Testament God blesses the poor and humble people. Apparently what was viewed as a blessing in the Old Testament is viewed as a danger in the New. *It is as if God discovers that his people cannot handle great wealth without the potential for great character disorders to develop.* These disorders make fools of people and deflect them from the main purposes and enjoyments of life. The economic structures of life tend to absorb everything. Then we come to the irreducible common denominator: *death* itself. We sacrifice much joy for very little that we can "take with us."

Jesus tells us the stories of a couple of fools. One has servants who wait on his every need. This man has a visitor every day — a man named Lazarus. Lazarus is a beggar. He stays alive by eating the pieces of bread which fall from the rich man's table. In that day bread was used as we would use a fine napkin. People wiped the gravy and food from their chins with chunks of bread and tossed them on the floor. Those scraps were Lazarus' food.

Now, the rich man was not a mean man. He was not cruel. He did not drive Lazarus from his door. Being rich was not his sin. His sin was that he possessed a character disorder: *he was indifferent to human need and he gave no thought to a final day of reckoning.* Consequently, he became indifferent to God. He was a *fool.* You see, the word Jesus uses for "fool" through his teachings is from the Psalms: "The fool says in his heart there is no God." The word, then, means a person who does not deny the existence of God but is indifferent to God — someone who commits no overt sin but just lacks feeling as to what life is all about. That's the difference between a sinner and a fool! *A sinner has done a wrong act. A fool has a fundamental character disorder.*

One can see this most keenly in the parable of the man Jesus directly called a "fool". The parable is about a man who once again let his riches blind him to everything except himself. The parable of the rich fool contains only sixty words. Yet the words, "I" and "my" occur twelve times. Listen to the egotism: "What shall *I* do, for *I* have nowhere to store *my* crops?' And he said, '*I* will do this: *I* will pull down *my* barns, and build larger ones; and there *I* will store all *my* grain and *my* goods. And *I* will say to *my* soul, Soul, you've done well.' "

Here is a person who has completely lost the capacity to say "we" and "our." He suffered from the cancerous character disorder of egotism. He became indifferent to his good fortune and thought of himself as a real self-made man. Social and financial categories became the basis of his self-pride.

All of us are dependent on God, not ourselves, for everything we have. The more I live the less I value people because of their social position. I have a friend who experienced the birth of a child the exact day our son, Scott, was born. Her child was born with an incurable disorder which affects the nerves. The child's body is paralyzed and soon it will die from the disease. Tens of thousands of dollars have been spent by those parents on the child. Thus a person every bit as bright and energetic as I would like to think I am finds herself buried for eight years under a mountain of medical bills and an incredible time commitment. It has greatly affected the social category to which the family belongs. But they have a spiritual richness I may never attain. All Jesus is saying is that a fool is a person who fails to recognize there are economic circumstances over which none of us individually has full control. *Our* barns are not just *our* barns because we were superior people. *Life has a very fragile quality to it and we must never forget that.*

Notice that Jesus calls the rich fool a dead man, spiritually. "Fool, this night your soul is required of you; . . ." When you fail to keep a line of distinction between the means by which you live and the ends for which you live, your soul dies. Even though you haven't ceased to breathe, you are spiritually dead.

A wealthy person who owned a mountain took a friend up to a lofty elevation on his property. They stood out on a deck overlooking the rich man's vast holdings, and the host quoted a phrase which is repeated on T-shirts sold at the beach: "You can tell the winners from the losers by the number of toys they leave behind when they die."

The further question, of course, is this: "But when do you really die?"

Was the winner Lazarus or the rich man? Temporal life is short. Eternal life is long. Life on earth is up and down with numerous additions and decreases. But like musical chairs, it doesn't matter how many are in the game with you, or how much has been given or taken away in the interim. All that matters is whether or not you have a place to sit when the music stops. Hope based on outward circumstances is a fleeting hope.

17

Hope in the Balance: Idealism and Realism

One of the hardest things to do in life is to live on the cutting edge between realism and optimism. Trying to balance these opposites, or at least hold them together in a living blend, is difficult. Idealists are not usually realistic. And the realists are not usually idealistic. Yet Christianity is a religion of balance. From the very beginning, the star and the stable were both part of the story. Life is not all star. And those wild-eyed optimists who followed the star in the heavens at some point had to give up that idealism to deal with the reality of a baby in an animal barn. But life is not all stable, either. At some point those realists who faced head-on the little baby had to enthusiastically invest themselves in the hope of the Kingdom of God being ushered in.

Have you ever stopped to think how the Christian faith is actually a belief in God's ability to work through incredible opposites? The star and the stable. The wisemen and the shepherds. The Rich Man and Lazarus. Peter and Judas. Paul the persecuter and Stephen the Stoned. The cross and the resurrection. Heaven and hell! The Jews and the Samaritans. The God strong enough to surround us with justice yet gentle enough to embrace us with grace. Incredible opposites. Jesus told his disciples they must simultaneously possess the characteristics of the serpent and the dove. "Be wise as serpents, and harmless as doves."

It's as if Jesus is saying "in order to determine the 'real thing' in life you must reconcile the kind of opposite extremes that infest and infect human life." Consequently, *every Christian must act for God out of both emotion and knowledge, idealism and realism, optimism and pessimism.*

I think it's harder to hold these opposites in tension today than ever before. Look at the confusion on television. Some of the preachers throw out a lot of heat but not much light. Emotionalism abounds.

But other prophets of doom emphasize special knowledge. All the esoteric philosophies and forecasts of reality really get me down. If the Russians will destroy us anyway or nuclear war will occur if the peace freezeniks don't prevail, why should I even bother to wallpaper my bathroom?

How does one become wise like the serpent but harmless like the dove? How to balance emotion and knowledge so as to live a hopeful life?

For much of my early life I lived on emotion and enthusiasm. Most of my teachers, coaches, and preachers thought emotion was the central essence of experience. It was drilled into my head that nothing significant is ever achieved without enthusiasm. In particular I remember our highly successful high school football coach, a motivation expert *par excellence*. In terms of backslapping, jumping around and thinking positive thoughts we outenthused everyone we played. We had tremendous camaraderie. An especially successful gimmick involved having the ball carriers growl just as soon as they touched the ball. This got the adrenalin flowing. And that same approach worked wonders in our churches. We had some youth revivals which compressed a lifetime of decisionmaking into a long Saturday night. You were afraid of being left out if you didn't get the zeal for Christ. Those forms of experiences that make you tingle and get goosebumps inside were everywhere.

But one day in college I had another revelation. It was my privilege to continue with athletics. For most of the month of August my first year our freshman team had been preparing for its initial scrimmage against the varsity. Since the varsity's first game was with Clemson University, all we had learned were Clemson's plays. We were an eager group, bringing with us the enthusiastic traditions of many high schools. We grouped together, screaming and charged-up. On the very first play our quarterback, with great confidence, took the snap from center and gave me the ball. I took the handoff and ran off tackle, growling as I had done in high school. Now in high school we usually just ran to the open area. So I never learned to pay attention to the defensive alignment or the quarterback's call of the defense. A huge, well-disciplined linebacker filled the hole. He slammed me in the chest, knocked my helmet off and gave me a cut above the eye that took five stitches to close. As he helped me up, he said, "Kid, you better quit growling and learn how to run the ball." As I wobbled back to the huddle I was painfully aware of a truism: while nothing significant is achieved without enthusiasm, *you are in real trouble if enthusiasm is all you have.* Nothing is achieved if all you have is well-intended idealism.

Jesus of Nazareth knew this. He knew it would take insight as well as enthusiasm to walk with God. Such was the meaning behind his parables of the tower builder and of the king preparing for war. Jesus issued a warning against any light-hearted assumptions. Jesus possessed some caution. Enthusiasm without realism can hurt you. Jesus said, know what you are getting into. Count the long-term costs. Consider your resources before you lay the foundation for a building. Otherwise, you will become an object of ridicule.

Jesus isn't appealing to fear of failure. He is not appealing for low achievement. But he apparently is afraid of mere emotion and idealism. Failure to finish something brings the kingdom into disrepute. Life and its battles are long and hard. Compulsive involvement is not the only human capacity needed for life.

For example, Paul wrote to the church in Rome, "I bear them witness that they have a zeal for God, but it is not enlightened." Paul knew from his own life as an enthusiastic persecuter of Christianity that emotion focused on improper ends is a horrible disease. *When religion becomes exclusively emotional and has no interest in knowing anything, it ceases to be a religion. It becomes a manic-depressive cycle.*

But God *has* given us feelings. And those feelings are an important part of Christianity. No great church was ever built on mere knowledge, spit, and tradition. At some point enthusiastic people, fired by a vision, have to want to share their life in Christ with others. In order to stay alive in Christ, you have to not only receive the good news of Christ but pass it on. Life comes from sharing a God whose message is one of victory and growth. Most everyone who is a member of a church is there because someone invited them. Religion without enthusiasm becomes cold and abstract and isolated from anything anyone would want to join. Religion without idealism is dead. It becomes afraid to plan. It knows too much knowledge to plan, to risk, to visualize. Instead of becoming wild-eyed "fools" for Christ or mustard seeds on the grow, we can become well-informed, nonrisking, cooly-calculated, "indifferent" realists. Jesus said, "When you try to save your life, when you play it safe, that's when you actually lose it."

The story is told[19] of a stranger who stopped for a drink of water at a farmhouse. He wanted to be sociable to the old barefooted farmer on the porch of the tumbledown shack. So he said, "How is your cotton coming?" "Ain't got none. Afraid of boll weevils," said the farmer.

"How is your corn?" said the stranger. "Didn't plant none. Afraid it wouldn't rain." replied the farmer. "Well, how about your potatoes?" "Ain't got none. Powerful lot of potato bugs in these parts."

"Well, what did you plant?" asked the bewildered stranger. "Nothin'," replied the farmer. "I'm just playin' it safe."

Jesus put it in terms of some people who were given different amounts of talents to work with. You'll remember that one man buried his in the ground, afraid he would lose it. I'll guarantee you, like the farmer in the tumbledown shack, any Christian and any church can find a hundred valid reasons not to venture anything. Enthusiasm is a part of the collective need of a church. Jesus said that if we do not possess it we become like "whitened tombs, which indeed appear beautiful outward, but are within full of dead men's bones."

But what about knowledge? Who wants to belong solely to a community of religious specialists? For example, there were people in the church at Corinth who felt the *knowing* aspect of Christianity was what really mattered. They were "up" on the latest details of religious theories or "down" on those people who did not believe exactly as they did. Apparently they became excited about subjects like bodily resurrection and what heaven is like.

Paul rather quickly let these people know that love is not boastful or rude. Love does not insist on its own way. After all, Jesus said, "People will know you by your love for each other." He did not say, "People will know you by your knowledge of esoteric doctrines." One certainly does not need a doctorate in theology to read, appreciate, and understand the Bible.

But Jesus the Christ understood full well the importance of knowledge. He called us to love God with our mind as well. He warned against those who would come and lead people astray by false teaching. In fact, Jesus asserted that an act of loving cannot be fully realized without a high regard for the mind. Our Scriptures were set in a particular culture. All Scriptures are interpreted to us by someone. And there are plenty of people in today's world willing to interpret the Scriptures for us — very eager to tell us what they know. You have to be careful whom you listen to.

John Claypool relates the delightful story of the famous Mexican bank robber, Jorge Rodriguez.[20] Jorge kept slipping across the Texas border and robbing banks. It got so bad the Texas Rangers deployed a whole posse to stop Jorge. One afternoon a Ranger spotted Jorge slipping across the Rio Grande and proceeded to trail him to his hometown. Jorge went into the cantina to relax. The Ranger slipped in, put a revolver to Jorge's head, and said: "I know who you are, Jorge Rodriguez, and unless you give me all the money you have stolen from Texas banks, I am going to blow your brains out." But Jorge did not understand English, and the Texas Ranger did not speak Spanish. About that time a little Mexican walked up and said, "I'm bilingual. I'll translate for you." He put the Ranger's proposition in language Jorge could understand. Jorge answered, "Tell the big policeman that I have not spent the money. If he will go to the town well, face north and count down five stones, he will find the money behind that stone." The little Mexican turned with a smile and said to the Ranger, in English, "Jorge Rodriguez is a brave man. He says he is ready to die!"

What you don't know can hurt you! Adolph Hitler knew that. In *Mein Kampf* he asserted:

"By means of shrewd lies, unremittingly repeated, it is possible to make people believe that heaven is hell and hell, heaven . . . the greater the lie, the more readily will it be believed."

Yes, idealism and emotion must always stand before the judgments of realism and truth.

Within the human being God has brought together in a powerful marriage the forces of emotion and knowledge, idealism and realism. In our life with Christ we must never pull asunder what God has joined together.

When we try to hold together enthusiasm for Christianity and sound knowledge about Christianity, we can live by covenant instead of conflict. We can be wise as serpents and harmless as doves.

18

Living In Covenant:
Hope in the Face of Broken Promises

William Brown is a friend of mine. You may not know William Brown, but I am glad I do. Brown is a world-class tenor. He was the first performer to sing in concert before an integrated audience in South Africa, an audience which he insisted upon. He has twice performed in Carnegie Hall in New York. *Ebony* magazine listed him among the prominent voices of the 80's. But William Brown is as important to me for his lifestyle, which radiates hope in God, as he is as a world-renowned tenor.

Perhaps the best way to indicate his approach to life is to recount for you a story. Perhaps you remember all too well the total chaos that existed in this country in the late 1960's and early 1970's. Values were in conflict, national conscience was pricked and lifestyles were in confusion. Cities were rocked with demonstrations and ugly violence. Confrontations were everywhere.

In the 1968-69 concert season, the then young 31 year old William Brown was scheduled to perform on the campus of Howard University in Washington, DC. The concert was sold out. But two days before the concert, Washington became a city under siege. Picket lines were all over the place. Riots and vandalism erupted with the slightest provocation. People were afraid to be out on the streets. On top of that, it began to rain on the evening of the concert. Every music critic scheduled to attend the concert cancelled out. They, like others, were afraid to venture out into the evening.

At the time the concert was to begin, *there were five people*, four women and one elderly gentleman, sitting as the audience in the concert hall which held 1800 people. Five people in a place that seated 1800! You can imagine the environment.

The pianist who was to accompany Mr. Brown said, "surely you're not going to go out there and give a concert performance! There are only five people out there. Let's go home."

Mr. Brown's response went like this. "Of course, I'm going to sing. Those people braved bad weather and picket lines to get here. I have a contract, a covenant, with them. One thing my father taught me is to always do your best when you have an obligation to fulfill."

And perform he did. It is a part of his covenant with life to perform. One wintry morning Brown was to sing in my church in North Carolina. The roads were almost impassable with ice and snow. I lamented the conditions to him but he imparted his philosophy to me: "I am here and I am in covenant. If only one person comes on Sunday we will make that person feel glad he or she came, for we will give our best." As it turned out, we had a packed house. But it really didn't matter to the performer.

That's quite a perspective, really, to live life according to a covenant to serve rather than be in conflict with what is, what was, or what might be. Imagine how strong a church would be if it so embraced a covenant with God to serve those who came that everyone, regardless of attendance, was always made to feel that they were especially welcomed. *I firmly believe there are higher loyalties beyond visible factors and finances.* If one has entered into covenant with God to live life in service of the Kingdom of God, one puts the same energy, the same pride, and the same time into one's work whether the crowd is 50 or 500.

The history of the Christian faith, of course, is a history of promises, or covenants; a history of promises kept and promises broken. The term covenant in our Scriptures means a solemn promise made binding by an oath which may be verbal or symbolic. What is true in Scripture stands unchallenged in the affairs of humankind: *The vast majority of human problems arise because individuals fail to keep their promises.*

It is impossible for us to understand our faith without visualizing it as a history of promises between humans and God. The covenant of Moses contained promises people made to do certain things for God in appreciation for what God had already done for them. In typical human fashion, no sooner were the promises made than those same people began to break them. Consequently, great emphasis had to be placed upon the divine forgiveness, and that became the foundation of the New Covenant predicted by Jeremiah. Jesus spoke of himself as the New Promise, poured out in his blood, to cover all the past *broken* promises between people and God.

Jesus entered into an agreement with us. He said, "I'll give you eternal life. Life forever. Something beyond this earthly existence. There is a place where all misery is wiped out, all pain dissipated, all despair thwarted — *forever*. A place with many houses for you to live in — *forever*."

"All you have to do to keep your end of the contract is to live a life of service to your fellow men and women." That's the agreement, service to humankind instead of *conflict* with humankind. No one can doubt what is laid upon us for our end of the bargain. Consider the parable of the good Samaritan or that more solemn utterance, where the dead stand before the throne of God dependent on whether they had fed the hungry, clothed the naked, given drink to the thirsty, and visited the imprisoned and the sick. "He that is greatest among you shall be your servant." That's a pretty straight-forward assessment, isn't it?

Those who are in covenant with God live a life of service. It doesn't matter if you're given the opportunity to serve one or one thousand — you serve that one or that thousand to your utmost.

The statement is obvious: *no one individual possesses enough resources to cope with all of life by himself or herself.* Mutual hope was the process from the very beginning. Hope is not an isolated affair. Without mutuality we die; we are unfulfilled, not whole. Hope is not a disembodied ideal. *Mutual service and involvement of persons create hope.*

The apostle Paul seems to tersely sum up the spirit of the whole New Testament in these words: "We that are strong ought to bear the infirmities of the weak and not to please ourselves." (Romans 15:1)

On some terms you must make a pact, a covenant, with God, to live your life serving others and letting them serve you. If not, your life will be one of continually resolving matters by conflict. *Why?* Why is a marriage not based on mutual self-giving in trouble? Why is a life that has not been given over to service a life in jeopardy? *Why must you and I live in service?*

It's simple: popular interpretations of the Declaration of

Independence to the contrary notwithstanding, human beings are *not* born completely equal in every respect. Partners in a marriage, members of a church, members of a family, neighbors on a street, employees in an office are not equal in *every* way. *All* are powerful in some respect and *all* are weak in other respects. A covenant of service is the only way the weak and the strong elements can live together on this earth. Without the ability to trust other people to fill-in the gaps in our personalities, you and I are incredibly impotent.

Consider the obvious state of affairs. People are not equal in practical ability. Some con operate with a great deal of practical efficiency while some of us are better at creativity and planning. People are not equal in intellectual capacity. Some people possess innate and learned wisdom about many things while others among us are contented, and rightly so, with not venturing into those unchartered waters. People are not equal in spiritual capacity. While all of us have in us the power to open up our lives to the Spirit of God through meditation and prayer, some of us are thimbles and others among us, oceans in comparative capacity. People are not equal in their understanding of social issues. Some of us relate religion to the great social needs of the time, while others among us view religion primarily as saving our own spiritual hide.

We need to covenant with rather than have conflict with humankind because *the greatest tragedy in life is not death. It is what we allow to die within us while we still live. It is the loss of hope.*

We rise or fall on the basis of our "convenants", our promises to serve one another. We live in a church because we have covenanted to help each other adjust our loads in life and carry them in the easiest manner. God calls us to live with certain burdens. We can't take these burdens off our shoulders, place them in a pile at the front of the church, and walk out of here leaving them behind forever. I wish we could, but we can't. Nor can we completely swap burdens with one another. We have to shoulder most of them ourselves. But we can form a "covenant" community in the service of God and others. Individually we are impotent, even to deal with ourselves. But in community there is every resource needed to adjust everyone's load to make it easier for all to carry on with their living. Think about that. A covenant to service each other instead of conflict with each other is the secret of productivity in any realm. William Rainey Harper is correct: *The question before us is how to become one spirit, not necessarily one in opinion."* Opinions change over the years according to external pressures and circumstances. *If all we develop here are common opinions we are in trouble.* But a unity of spirit is an incredible achievement of lasting promise.

If we can make everyone around us feel welcomed, regardless of their opinions; if we can make our neighbors here feel glad they know us and always put out our best effort at service as our end of the bargain for what God has done for us in Jesus Christ, covenant, not conflict, will result. People of various opinions who now wander in doubt searching for light will find an anchor and a rock and a resting place in our hope in Christ. People who feel bitter and angry at seemingly unfair differences of society will begin to regard the world in a gentler, more humble, and more tender spirit. Their hope in the God of the mutual responsibility will be awakened.

In Christianity we safely dispense with many things. But the covenant between God and humankind, which affirms that the highest strength should be put at the service of the lowest weakness, is the central pillar of the gospel. The true test of our hope is the point below which it allows the weaknesses and frailities of our neighbors to fall.

Life is lived by covenant. Without that, there is little hope. Living within the covenant God makes with us, a new and vibrant future waits for us.

19

Facing Old Age Hopefully

Recently, I had an opportunity to return to a place I had not visited in fifteen years, Ridgecrest Baptist Assembly in Ridgecrest, North Carolina. As part of that experience I visited its bookstore. Everything looked pretty much the same as I had remembered it, with one notable exception. Apparently a new line of materials has been added to the glamour books written by the pastors of large churches, the Miss Americas, and the movie stars. The spiritual records collection now contains an incredible number of albums and tapes for Christian aerobics and "Christian" exercise dancing. That's really amusing to me because Ridgecrest Assembly still doesn't allow "real" dancing between couples on its grounds. And even Baylor University, largest of all Baptist universities and supreme protector of Southern Baptist social values, still doesn't allow "real" dancing on campus.

Now this is not a treatise against dancing. There are at least eight different forms of dancing before the Lord in the Old Testament, and I believe that most churches would be healthier and happier if they had more dances. What I am trying to say is that as Christians we seem to have an easier time finding God in potential efforts to "cheat the aging process" than in finding and celebrating God in the aging process itself. This seems to me to be a real deficiency. You see, the only thing all of us have in common is the fact tht we are growing older, admittedly at different rates of speed. Time stops for no one. When God created this earth, aging was a part of that creation. And we humans haven't really looked for God in that process. Indeed, we have tended to look for God in trying to get out of that process. Such accounts for much of our despair in a modern technological society which has prolonged the aging process, including the act of dying itself.

Centuries ago a Spanish explorer name Ponce de Leon went so far as to suggest the existence of a fountain of youth whose magical waters possessed the ability to renew the body and make it young again. And, truthfully, I think the "Ponce de Leon" anxiety will be with us forever since aging is a built-in ingredient to the human condition. Sometimes our entire culture appears to believe that Shakespeare was correct in describing us as merely poor players who strut and fret our hour upon the stage of life and then are heard from no more. We certainly appear to be trying to get all the strutting and fretting in while we can.

If there is a fundamental need in our lives, it appears to be *the need to celebrate God in the aging process and live life in the presence of the eternal instead of crowding it out in favor of the temporary.*

One of the hallmarks of our culture seems to be a crowding out of things that really matter by things that do not matter much. All of us, myself especially, tend to so fear growing older that we are becoming absorbingly busy with trivialities. We do not disbelieve the might and power of God, but we simply don't have room for God. We practically crowd God out of our lives. We miss the primary duty of life, what Jesus Christ called "putting first things first and letting everything else fall into place." Think about this. Jesus Christ appears never to have met an atheist. He really did not have to deal with nonbelievers. He ministered to many fine people who had become so preoccupied with other things, even religious trivialities, that they had crowded out of their life a personal relationship with God. Frankly, the pressing problem in our day just may be the fact that *many of our people just don't* have time for God.

It has never been so easy to fail in this particular way as it is today. There may have been times in rural American society when life was sluggish and people could drift listlessly through the seasons, at harmony with nature and meditation and prayer, cultivating the emotions and senses as well as the business of production. But if that time ever existed, it is gone. Today life is swift. Its currents are stimulating. There are more things to do than we shall ever get done; there are more toys to play with than we shall ever be able to buy; there are more avenues for enjoyment than we shall ever find time to travel. We are tempted to live not bad but frittered lives — split and scattered. Preoccupation is such a common form of failure that *we view eternal life or heaven as something beginning after death because it's only then we will have time to crowd it in.*

Amazingly enough, Jesus saw this as a fundamental human problem as long ago as two thousand years. Perhaps the least understood words of Jesus are these from Matthew's 22nd chapter: "And as for the resurrection, have you not read . . . He is not the God of the dead, but of the living." The God of the living; not the God who comes at death. When we put first things first and begin a primary, personal relationship with God, eternal life begins then. It continues long after the physical body has been shed. Consequently, aging for such a person is a moving *toward* that for which we were created in the first place instead of a moving *away from* something, youth and physical vigor, which should be preserved at all costs.

In fact, our Bible is simply a record of the total contrast between aging without God and aging with God. And, really, that's our choice: choose life or choose death. "I have set before you life and death. Choose life," are the words of God in Deuteronomy. "Choose those things that are eternal where dust and rust and the things of this world cannot get at them, or choose the temporal things of this world which will rust and rot and be destroyed," said Jesus. Be born into eternal life and grow toward even more life and fulfillment, or be born and gradually watch all you have accumulated be turned to dust, including your own body.

In order to make a success of life, much less make a success of old age, *most of us must begin now to find the God in our aging process.* We must reorganize our existence with an eye toward our eternal nature instead of becoming preoccupied by our rather temporary social and professional whirls. It is what Jesus called "being born again" or having new eyes with which to see and new ears with which to hear.

Paul Tournier, in his book, *Learning to Grow Old,* notes:

*Success in any undertaking always demands
some training, the establishment of reflexes
and habits, and some ability, if not a
proper apprenticeship, and these things do
not come easily at a more advanced age if they
have not been started earlier (p.18).*

What happens to most of us during our active and preoccupied careers as business or professional people, parents, housekeepers and providers is that we encourage certain productive facets of ourselves to meet the needs and obligations of these years. But we similarly lose touch with many other facets of our being. Like instruments unplayed for many years, these emotions grow out of tune and become remote to us.

The highest is in us all. At times it flames up and we feel the spirit of God in all its power and peace. We touch base with some of those unplayed instruments from God like family love, enriching friendships, constant prayer and daily meditation. But we run past that field of life in our quest to cram all the productive things in before we get to the end of life.

But *our life is not a field to be run past. It is a garden to be tilled and grown.* We cannot be so preoccupied with running past the field that we either forget to plant the fruit or let the weeds grown out the seeds God has planted in us.

That is the consistent metaphor throughout the Scripture. Genesis 2:8 tells of our creation in these words: "And the Lord God planted a garden eastward in Eden, and there he put the human whom he had formed." The prophet Jeremiah contended that his people's soul would be as "a watered garden and they (would) not sorrow any more at all."

And after all the prophecies were fulfilled and Jesus was crucified, Joseph of Arimathea placed his body in a garden. And, you will remember when Mary Magdala came to the tomb of the risen Christ she mistook Jesus for the gardener. The Scriptures are quite clear: *life is not a field to be run past. It is a garden to be tilled and grown.* If you can embrace that philosophy you can celebrate God in our process of aging.

Luke's account of the infancy of Jesus contains a beautiful narrative about a prophetess, Anna, the daughter of Phannel, of the tribe of Asher. She was a very old woman who had tilled, watered, and tended the garden of her soul throughout the long years of her life. Her life had been one of constant prayer and devotion. She apparently had not succumbed to the temptation to preoccupy herself with trivialities. And her style of living paid off for her. Her training, her reflexes and her habits brought her into a proper relationship with God. And in old age she was reaping the harvest of a spiritual garden well attended.

We are given the assurance by Jesus that we can trust him to stay close to us when we try to find time to cultivate our spiritual life in the midst of a busy world. It's hard to relax and make time for God when you're worried about what will happen to your job, your reputation or your income if you do. But Jesus' promise is clear: "I will not leave you orphans; I will come back to you . . . because I live, you will live . . . Anyone who receives my commandments and keeps them will be one who loves me; and anybody who loves me will be loved by my father and I shall love that person and show myself to him or her." (John 14:18-21)

"I will not leave you orphans; I will come back to you" — is there any greater security? It means we need not worry about life, even losing it. We need not worry about certain things that represent life to us — our jobs, our loved ones, our reputations. We stay concerned about those things. But we are no longer frantic about them. Their absence will not destroy us. We can live under a sense of gracefulness instead of compulsiveness. You see, that which matters most will crowd out those things which do not matter as much. Eternal life will have begun. And we will never be an orphan. We will be moving *toward* that for which we were created and which gives us meaning.

20

Hope When There Seems Not Be Any: Confronting Suicide

I once traveled in a police car one hundred fifty-three miles in less than one hour and twenty minutes. I was in the car with two police officers and a psychiatrist. We drove to I-85, and the race against time began. Seldom have I been so frightened. The policemen turned on the flashing lights and pushed the car as fast as it would go. We were going so fast that when we went over little dips in the road the ashtray would pop down and spray ashes in the air, like a gray snowfall. Once when the psychiatrist asked me to see how fast we were traveling, I looked at the speedometer. It only registered to 130 miles per hour and the needle was buried to the right of that. We didn't look anymore.

Finally, we arrived at the lake where a fiend of mine had a second home. Nervously the psychiatrist and I walked toward the boat dock. There he was, a friend in desperation, standing by the lake with a shotgun pointed at his head. With seemingly everything to live for, he had chosen death because he was afraid of life. Suicide had become the constant focus of his life, making everything else irrelevant, a diversion. Every sporadic burst of work, each minor disappointment and success, seemed but a temporary calm on a steady descent through layers of depression, like an elevator stopping briefly on its way down to the basement. He had tried every way he knew to get off or change the direction of the journey. But nothing had worked. He and his wife had spent the last five years of their marriage thrashing around, like two drowning persons pulling each other under.

Fortunately the experience had a fairly successful conclusion. It was my first experience with someone attempting suicide. It was hardly my last. At least once a month I counsel with someone who has attempted suicide. And all of us go through periods, in various degrees, when we wonder if we can really go on with what life demands. A school teacher struggles to muster the energy just to look at a mountain of papers on her desk. They are weeks overdue. A businessman sits in his car for an hour unable to turn the key in the ignition and go to work. A lawyer locks himself in his office for hours at a time. A homemaker noted for hard work and tidiness finds herself unable to plan a meal or do the dishes and sits in her bathrobe from breakfast until the afternoon, staring out the window at nothing. A minister from whom sermon ideas usually flow like a mountain stream after a heavy rain sits in front of a blank legal pad unable to write a single sentence. A high school student who has the capability of making good grades is suddenly paralyzed in the face of life and thinks she will not be able to graduate.

Eventually such people begin to have feelings of guilt and worthlessness, wondering if they will ever be able to cope with life. Call it burn-out. Call it depression. Call it what you will. "To be depressed is, very simply, to be stopped short in one's life."[21] *There comes a time when the demands for living seem to be greater than the resources we have.* Such was the experience of the prophet Elijah, a man who suffered from waves of depression. After one of his bouts with depression, Elijah was led by God into hiding by the brook of Cherith, east of the Jordan. Ravens brought him bread and meat, and he drank from the brook. But then his supplies for life began to dwindle. Imagine the anxiety as he watched the trickle of water growing less and less. Then one morning the brook completely dried up. The prophet must have been a pitiful sight as he went to the home of a widow and, in rags and tags, barely clinging to life, said, "Please bring me a little water to drink and a little meat to eat." Amazingly, some days later, this same prophet blessed the household and even took her ailing son to an upper chamber and healed him. Now, how could this man who found life running out on him suddenly make a 180° turn and become a person of power? How could this person recover from a parched season in his life and turn from a suicidal prophet into a champion for life? And how can we, like the widow in Zarephath, help that process for other people? *There must be a way to affirm the sixth day of creation.*

According to the Genesis account, God created humankind on the sixth day, in the image of God. He gave us dominion over the earth, and voiced that it had been a very good thing to have done. In spite of the fact that each year half a million people in the U.S. attempt suicide and it is now the third leading cause of death among adolescents, God said the sixth day was good.

Understanding suicide is a key to preventing it. Perhaps the first feeble step is your willingness to read this chapter. John White, Professor of Psychiatry at the University of Manitoba, writes: "I have listened to hundreds, indeed thousands, of sermons, but never one on suicide."[22] Indeed, it is a hushed subject. But the Bible is not afraid of it. The Bible chronicles five suicides and serves as the oldest recorded statement of depression (King Saul). In addition, Jesus met many people whose brooks had dried up, whose *resources* for living were not adequate for the *tasks* of living. Such people were committing suicide by degrees, slowly. We humans tend to do that even in our cigarettes, alcohol, stress, and obesity. Jesus himself screamed from the cross, "My God, my God, why have you forsaken me." The anguish of betrayal, sacrifice, and loneliness weighed on his life, too.

The entire Christian faith is, in a sense, devoted to death. Death is the first concern of the soul. *Man was created as a creature who can betray his own best interests.* That's the way God made us. God also made us so we can relate our lives to his purposes and find forgiveness for our sins and the strength to rebuild shattered lives. How, then can we help?

In the first place, we can extend to those who have felt the burden of suicide in their families *the God who never stops loving a person regardless of their frailties.* Many people think the early church taught that suicide, taking one's own life, was the unpardonable sin. They argue that our lives are not our own, since we are God's creatures. Suicide, then, is refusing God's world and setting up oneself in the seat of judgement. Actually, that teaching comes not from the Bible or the early church, but from St. Augustine in his *City of God.*[23] We are indeed God's creatures but we were created as creatures who can betray our own best interests. God made us that way and thought it was good. But God also sent his son to tell us the parable of the lost sheep. God is concerned not only with those inside the fold, living healthy lives and dying natural deaths; he is also interested in those who have strayed from life. Humans, like sheep, wander away from their own kind. Jesus said God doesn't go away and leave these misplaced persons. He does not condemn them to outer darkness. He goes after them and picks them up in his arms. Even when a person betrays life, God looks on whith tender pity and everlasting love. So we can help remove theological guilt.

We can also help a family remove psychological guilt. Often families think if only they had realized the person was mentally ill, they could have helped. Still other families feel guilty that they might have driven the person to become mentally ill. Well, only about one-third of the people who complete suicide could remotely be described as mentally ill.[24] In addition, there is no evidence that suicide is passed down genetically. It is a learned behavior. If it runs in the family, it is learned rather than inherited. We should certainly help families work through theological and psychological guilt.

What about prevention? How, like the widow at Zarephath, can we help prevent this destructive tendencey in our society? One-half to three-fourths of all suicides can be prevented. There aresome things we can do.

With adolescents we must, first of all, *confront romantic notions of death.* Adolescents fantasize themselves beautifully laid out like Snow White while everyone comes by to exclaim how great they are. They imagine themselves the center of attention. Since they are far away from death in illness and age, they often see it as a quiet sleep. But death is not a friend. As Paul says, "Death is the enemy." It is irreversible. Jesus has produced victory over the enemy, but it is still *enemy.* We should take every adolescent in the church on a tour of a funeral home's operations and take every young adult to the hospital to witness an autopsy. Death is not a friend.

Secondly, the church can keep solid its moral guidelines and its closely knit supportive networks. The influences which lead adolescents toward suicide are changing moral climates, high mobility, a high divorce rate, abuse of alcohol and other drugs, glorification of violence in the media, and the already high suicide rate. It is a documented fact that persons are more prone to suicide when the churches they attend no longer constitute a closely knit supportive network. As persons deal with the shock produced by abrupt changes in life, they must have some stable institution to lean on. As John White says, "A television set can never hug you."[25]

Closely tied to this point is another help we can be to people — *we can stop over-promising what life will be like*. We live in a world of *salespersons*. Much of what we do is geared to advertising. But, selling materials and commodities is quite different from selling promises about life. Our generation is the most over-expectant generation in history. Ministers can concentrate on selling the church, and gaining new converts, instead of producing service and quality ministries. And we reward the pastors who sell best. Consider even college. Most colleges have eight people in their admissions departments, *selling* students on the idea of coming there, for every one person they have in placement trying to help them get a job once they have been there. Life's visions, from what a young girl expects of marriage to what an adult sees in wealth, is like driving up to a car lot to buy a car — four salesmen will fight to get to you. Life's reality is like buying the car and coming back the next week to try to get an appointment to have it serviced. They will tell you you're number forty-two in line and to come back the next week. *Jesus never over-promised what life would be like.* In his beatitudes he started out with some blessings and ended up telling his followers what to expect — "blessed are you when people utter evil against you falsely, revile you, persecute you, etc., for so they did these things to the prophets before you." He says there are certain things you will have to live with, like the weather. There are some things that have had no answers throught the years and you just have to live with them. There are conditions in life we live with and there aren't any answers or magical solutions to them.

Churches can also help people trapped in negative thinking. People in depression get caught up in a triad of negatives: 1) a negative view of oneself; 2) a negative interpretation of one's experiences; and 3) a negative view of the future. Jesus tried to confront this triad. He taught love of self; he did not accept conclusions for which no grounds existed, whether it was people blaming parents for a person's blindness or the woman caught in adultery; and he certainly had a grand view of the future.

You see, you and I live in a world where praise is offered in whispers and criticism comes like thunderclaps. We need to reverse that trend. Good news doesn't stay with you minute to minute the way bad news does. We discount praise but register criticism full strength. Suppose you get a promotion. That makes you happy for a couple days. You celebrate. But you don't get up every succeeding morning and say, "I've been promoted." You come to depend on that satisfaction. It is the most fleeting pleasure you ever have. But compare it to being fired. You live with that misery day after day. And you feel socked in the stomach every time you think of it. We somehow need to discount failure and register praise full strength. You see, people do not necessarily become more self-confident the more successful or established they are. People can still be apprehensive about failing and now they have farther to fall. Competence is expected. At a certain point you can only stumble because you become compared with your best, competent self. Who praises a dentist for doing a good filling? Who thanks the accountant for filling out a tax return with no mistakes?[26] Who thanks a homemaker for a clean shirt? Probably very few do. You see, professionals reach competency and that's what we pay them to do. But let them mess up and wrath comes. Notice how even in the little things of life, from oil poured on his head to the woman who touched his garment, Jesus discounted failure and registered praise full strength.

Finally, when we encounter depressed persons, *we should discourage mere devotional reading and encourage Bible reading and study.* It doesn't help a depressed person to read Norman Vincent Peale, or Robert Schuller, or Zig Ziglar, or Harold Warlick. They need to read the Bible. I quote a medical doctor: "In most depressed people devotional reading has degenerated into something unhelpful and unhealthy." You see, people become even more depressed when they try to be like a particular motivational expert, wanting to know, "why it works for them and not for me!" But in the Bible there are abiding words of comfort and assurance that the depressed person can apply to his or her own world view without trying to copy someone else's world view. Such copying only leads to disappointment because the authors themselves are not the know-it-alls their books suggest. *Books are meant to be helpful, not to provide rescue. The Bible, on the other hand, brings God's own hopeful, rescuing, redeeming promises.*

In short, we can affirm the sixth day of creation. We can affirm a God of everlasting love for all people. We can confront romantic notions of death. We can keep our church unified and solid. We can refuse to over-promise what life will be like. We can discount failure and register praise full strength, for everyone including those high-achievers that we think don't need it. And we can encourage real Bible reading instead of mere devotional reading. In these ways we can perhaps do our part to prevent tragedy.

In fact, we can give hope where there seems not to be any. For the sake of *those in our midst* who are most bereft of hope, we dare do nothing less.

21

The Personal Touch:
Hoping In the God Who Knows Our Name

Each year certain congratulatory letters arrive in our home. One of these letters begins like this: "Congratulations, you have been recommended for biographical and pictoral inclusion in a volume of the *International Who's Who*. Please send a small paragraph for publication when you return your completed questionnaire." The computer-written form letter is accompanied by another letter notifying me that for "only" $150.00 (U.S.) I can obtain a royal edition of the book and read the small paragraph about myself. A cheaper paperback copy is available for "only" $50.00 (U.S.). Having learned my lesson two years ago, I immediately dispose of such letters. You see, two years ago I kept receiving a questionnaire every few months from a Who's Who publication that I did not wish to respond to. I kept throwing the inquiries in the trash can. Then, after some months had passed, I noticed the correspondence had ceased. I casually mentioned to my secretary at the time that I was delighted we were no longer receiving that "junk mail." "Oh, yes," she remarked, "I grew tired of handling that material, so one day about six months ago, I completed the form for you. I simply fabricated some data, in order to keep them from soliciting us."

Well, in panic I ran to the telephone and started calling my family. Alas, I was too late. My father had already purchased the $50.00 paperback. My aunt had also sent in her check. And even my wife's parents were contemplating a favorable response to the smashing news from the company.

In the United States local newspapers have had to run editorials warning high school students and their parents about such enterprises. One venture, *Who's Who Among High School Honor Students,* has made millions of dollars by simply deeming any student who responds to their questionnaire an "honor" student.

The success of such offers points to a salient fact in our world: regardless of our position or influence in life, at the basic level of existence, *all of us cry out for recognition.* It is a natural craving of the human heart to want to amount to something in the eyes of the world. We want to have the tap of recognition on our shoulders. We want the world to know that we are more than the sum total of our x-rays, blood tests, and urinalyses. We want the world to know that we are more than the sum total of our work and child bearing and rearing. We want a little feeling of being touched or tapped or set apart or written about by somebody or some group that recognizes and affirms our importance.

In our day of computers and identification numbers set within the sprawling mass of big business, big government, and international communication, we are in some ways more isolated from meaningful human contact than any generation before us. Chores are no longer social events. Most of us do not buy commodities, food, and services from personal friends. And the product of our increased mobility has been a mixture of freedom and uprootedness. The average adult now moves fourteen times in his or her lifetime. Consequently, never have there been so many books on the market dealing with intimacy and loneliness. We shout the loudest where we hurt the most.

In the midst of such a world, it behooves us to go back to the record of the human discovery of the God we worship. In the 33rd chapter of Exodus, Moses is worried and goes before God. The people in his charge have just constructed a golden calf. They have sinned. And Moses doesn't know what's going to happen. Maybe God will leave them forever. Or, even worse, God might destroy the whole lot of them. So Moses seeks some assurance that God will stay with the people in spite of their foolishness. In response to the request, God gives this earth-shaking reply, "Moses, *I know you by name.*"

In that simple sentence came a new concept of God. A promise was made that the people of God would have a *personal* relationship with God. "I know you by your name." In an antiquarian society of dreams, visions, demons, and awesome terror, came a powerful new message. God is not detached from and uninterested in his creation. God can make himself small enough to know his children by name.

A particular insight into the personal aspect of God's nature was brought to us by Jesus Christ. Most of Jesus' teachings focused on the availability of a *personal*, caring God for each and every one of us. To be without the personal touch, whether by physical illness such as the lepers, by accident like a lost coin or a lost sheep, by willful action such as the Prodigal Son, or by anonymity such as the woman reaching for the garment, was the worst fate Jesus imagined for anyone.

A gentleman by the name of Fynn captured the essence of Moses' discovery and Jesus' teaching. He wrote a book called *Mister God, This is Anna*. Anna was a special little five year old girl whom Fynn had met. She possessed the incisive idea that Mister God, as she called him, did not at all mind making himself small. Her words were profound: "People who think that Mister God is very, very big make a big mistake. Mister God can be any size he wants to be." To be certain, my friends, we make a mistake if we assume that God is always to be found in bigness and power. God has throughout human history evidenced the concern and the love to make himself very small and personal. God is a God who lives at our elbow and knows our name.

In this Twentieth Century world of much loneliness and despair through feelings of lack of importance, there is a message for us. In a capsule, Jesus' message was that *God's nature is to love each of us as if there were but one of us to love.* We are all included in God's *Who's Who.* No one is left out.

We constantly concern ourselves a lot about "what we believe about God." Of equal importance is what God believes about us. God knows our name. Most people value Christ for his ethics, or his sacrificial death on the cross, or his extension of hope for eternal life through his resurrection. These emphases, of course, are of unquestionable importance. But it is also true that *no one has come to God as Father except in Christ.* Nowhere in Islam or Buddhism, Hinduism or Marxism do we find affirmed the ultimacy of the personal relationship of humans with God.

God indeed knows our name and prepares a personal place for each of us to live eternally with him. John's gospel quotes Jesus as saying, "I am the good shepherd; *I know my own sheep and they know me . . . ."* (10:14)

Jesus and, ultimately, God as our loving shepherd is one of the key concepts of the Bible. An incredible amount of personal love for sheep goes into being a good shepherd. I recently went to the home of a friend who owns some sheep to take a look at what's involved in being a shepherd. It's amazing how close and personal a relationship is involved in caring for sheep. Sheep are so docile they will not drink from swift running water. You can place sheep in a field near a roaring stream and they will die of thirst. They will let the life-giving water flow past them and never touch it, out of their fear. In such cases the shepherd must either build a still-water pool or hand-carry water to them in pans or bowls. If that were not incredible enough, consider this: a mother sheep will walk away from her babies and not feed them. The shepherd has to pick up the baby and hand carry it to the mother for it to eat. I watched a young lamb, born that morning stand bleating for food while the mother stood a few feet away looking placidly at something else. The little lamb would have starved to death if it had had to depend on the mother to move over a few feet. Finally, sheep are so docile that they don't even put up resistance when another animal attacks them. A dog can destroy an entire herd and the sheep won't even run.

For me, that backdrop is far more than the lifting of an agrarian motif from the past to the present. It is life as we know it. We sit in a pasture called earth with all the options available for living that anyone could ask for. Through the center of our existence runs a life-giving resource. But left on our own, running with our insecurities and fears, we would sit down and die of thirst only inches from real nourishment. So God, the good shepherd, brings the drink to us in a form that is more acceptable to us, a human being of peace and calmness, his son, the Christ.

Likewise we stand in a world of riches, where we have so much to offer one another and so many resources of food, clothing, kindness, and love to offer those less fortunate than we. Those countless folk stand only a few feet from us, bleating their heads off for a little of the life-giving resources we possess. If they had to depend on the natural goodness of our hearts to move us over a few feet to them, they would surely starve to death. So God says, "I will send you a shepherd to teach you that when these bleating lambs are carried to you, you'll know that when you feed the least of them you are really doing it unto me."

Similarly, we are left like sheep in the midst of a world of raging dogs. When the snarling teeth of greed, ugliness, pettiness, prejudice and warped religious leaders come running up to us, we often find it easier to offer no resistance than to fight. Any of these mad dogs of selfishness can clean us out and often we find our entire herd of fellow humans just standing there waiting with us for the ruin. Again, the good shepherd comes to our aid and puts up a fence called the "church." Inside this protective device we are supposed to find at the least a place to gather for a brief time each week, somewhat removed from the snarling hounds of a secular world.

The purpose of much of our New Testament was to tell the good news about this place where loving intimacy and personal relationships could develop between people. We are a Kingdom community, a place where every name is known by the good shepherd and every personhood is held equally precious. That's a strong affirmation to carry into life's trenches, isn't it? Affirmation carries a responsibility. We who are affirmed must carry the personal and caring touch to the desperate, hungry people who have been smitten by the world's greed and prejudice. To Simon Peter, Jesus posed the question, "Do you love me?" Then he offered the advice, "Well, if you love me, then feed my sheep."

What an affirming glimpse you and I have received into the personal love God has for us. From Moses through Christ it has shivered its way over five thousand years of human history. I thought of it most recently in hearing some events that transpired in a university city.[27]

A certain college was observing Visitors Day and the parents were invited to stay on the campus for some weekend activities. The local merchants were vying for the anticipated increase in business. A favorite watering hole among the students there was Larry's Tavern. That popular establishment also served a marvelous Sunday brunch. So two days before Visitors' Day, a huge advertisement appeared in the local paper. Its headline read: "Bring your parents to Larry's Tavern for Sunday brunch." At the bottom of the ad were these words: "p.s., I'll pretend I don't know you. Signed Larry."

The very next day, another huge ad appeared in the same paper. It was headlined: "Bring Your Parents to the College Chapel for

Worship Tomorrow." At the bottom of the ad were these words:
"p.s., I'll pretend I know you very well. Signed, the Chaplain."

To the prodigal sons and daughters, the lepers, the demoniacs,
the disciples, the rich young rulers, the ill-spirited, and to each of
us comes an advertisement which still thunders its way across the
gaps of recorded time: "Come to Me All of You Who Are Heavy
Laden and I will Give you Rest."

"p.s.. I don't have to pretend I know you, for I know you by
name. Signed, God."

p.p.s. That brings us to the end of our story.

Part Four

The End of Our Story

22

The Virtue of Hope: Taking Courage
When The World Turns Cowardly

An especially vivid memory revolves around my junior high school's science fair. Science fairs were a great deal of fun to us wide-eyed ninth graders. Every person who visualized himself as a potential scientist genius entered a homemade project. During the science fair of my ninth year in school, one exhibit held center stage: a student had taken a huge red apple and injected a fungus. The apple was placed on a little pedestal surrounded by posters narrating the progression of the fungus. There it sat, a huge shiny apple with a little fungus growing on one side of it.

As our class marched by the other exhibits, my mind continued to focus on that huge red apple. Finally, I could take it no more. My best friend, Melvin, and I drew away from the group and hurried back to the apple exhibit. At last I reached out and grabbed the apple. Opening my young mouth as wide as possible, I took a gigantic bite out of the heart of the apple. Then, I hastily replaced it on its pedestal. Needless to say, the shiny apple with its hole and teeth marks became the subject of great merriment on the part of our class.

The teacher, of course, did not find the event to be so amusing. Her scowling face indicated that the culprit, if caught, would be in serious trouble. She began an intense interrogation of each student. Finally, in utter exasperation, she declared, "I just wish the student who did this had the *courage* to admit it.

Well, when she implied that I possessed a lack of courage, the cat was out of the bag. She'd struck a vital nerve. "Who are you saying hasn't got any courage?" I retorted.

Lowering her eyes into an unforgetable stare, she addressed

me, "At least you're no fool. You've got some sense of virtue that can be appealed to."

Having expected the worst, I was somewhat taken back by her mild manner, She continued, "What you did was wrong. But your failure to confess to it would have been a greater wrong. To make an impulsive mistake is human, but to have no system of virtue that can be appealed to is tragic." In a strange way, the teacher rewarded me for my virtue instead of attacking me for the bad incident.

I've thought long about that lesson I learned early in life.

The great psychologist Karl Menninger has written a book entitled *Whatever Became of Sin?* He notes that in the early days there was no question as to the existence of sin, but today the word seems to have disappeared. Menninger calls us back to the word not for the sake of the word "sin" but for reintroduction of a concept of moral responsibility.

While acknowledging this thesis, we must go to the corresponding question: whatever became of virtue? After all, not sin, but foolishness is our real problem. Whatever became of virtue?

I think the news media, the newspapers, television, and the electronic evangelists have done a good job now in convincing us that Satan is alive and well on planet earth. Sin is available for viewing, reading and listening about from preachers to a phenomenal extent. In fact, most of us worry more about finding activities that will shield our children from sin than we do about cultivating within them the kind of virtues described by 2 Peter. We are more acquainted with sin than hope. Listen to what 2 Peter clicks off as an essential accompaniment to faith: knowledge, self-control, steadfastness, godliness, affection for one another, etc.

The moralists in ancient Greece and Rome adhered to four fundamental virtues — wisdom, justice, temperance, and courage. Christianity took over all four virtues, but realizing that these virtues speak chiefly to our relations to others and to our society, added three more: faith, hope and love.

I recently viewed a cartoon in a newspaper which embodied the concept of "positive reinforcement". A woman informed her husband that one of the family dogs had torn up the garage. The husband told her that he would take care of it and proceeded to walk outside. After a few minutes the woman ventured outside to see what progress was being made in punishing the delinquent dog. To her dismay her husband was petting the dog that had *not* created the damage. When questioned by his wife, the man responded, "Sometimes you have to show affection for the one who doesn't get into trouble."

Indeed, our constant attention to the problem person has an adverse affect on behavioral patterns. So few parents ever praise other adults. Most of us are insecure people who satisfy our ego needs through criticizing others. I once visited a young girl in jail who related to me that her parents never had a kind word to say about anyone. All her life she had heard the minister, the police, the school principal, her teachers, and the significant adults around her criticized. Over a period of years her mind absorbed the negativism, and when she became a teenager she had no positive valuations formed. Her protection in life was to always find self-esteem through finding something to criticize. Her life was lived with no hope of finding trustworthy human beings. Without hope and trust at the human level it is hard to have hope and trust in God. Through a process of transference virtually all authority figures are seen as hopeless.

There are two pieces of advice I once was given that force you to labor under my pen. One of my best friends, now deceased, Grady Nutt, told me that the act of preaching is essentially "one beggar telling another beggar where he found bread." So I have always viewed the art as a sharing of one's story. Another valued friend told me that preaching is confessional, so in the first year and a half that you are in a church you share who you are with the people so that, agree or not, like it or not, they at least understand the personality through which you are communicating. Then they can help you with it or at least sympathize with it. Since I have not been in a new parish that length of time, I may be over-zealous in laying bare my soul.

I do not understand casual commitments or convenient relationships. I do not understand a casual commitment to one's promises, one's job, one's vocation, or one's church. I do not understand yielding to avoidance of hard work, individuality, or creative leadership by blending in with the herd, a phenomenon psychologists call "protective coloring." I do not understand people who look for that which is most convenient at the cost of surrendering their steadfastness to their covenants. Perhaps I was born too poor, became too agressive somewhere along the line or have

142

residues of outmoded and old fashioned thinking. I view the Bible as a series of covenants or promises poured out to cover all the past broken promises on the part of people. But it is a new covenant in his blood, a new promise, not the substitution of a belief in promises by a belief in casual commitments.

In *A Man For All Seasons* the story is told of Sir Thomas More and his battle to maintain an oath he had taken to the church. For me, it is one of the classic stories in the human legacy. In the most gripping moment of the story, Sir Thomas stands defiantly before his adversaries and proclaims, "When a man takes an oath, he holds himself in his own hands like water. When he opens, all that he has and all that he is slips away."

I think that's the most important thing a person can teach, the ability to keep your word and be steadfast — not stubborn or naive, just steadfast, hopeful. It's that quality exhibited so many times by Jesus and captured in Luke's 12th chapter when he spoke: "Fear not little flock, it is your father's good pleasure to give you the kingdom. Give what you have, point toward a treasure in the heavens that does not fail, where no thief will ever approach and no moth destroy."

Now, I guess that's Jesus' way of saying nice guys and nice girls do not finish last in the sight of God. Finding some courage, steadfastness, hope, fortitude, or resiliency within you to hang onto is a strength. In fact, Jesus time and time again seems to have indicated that the presence of one brave, virtuous person can always and everywhere be a strength and an inspiration to show that virtue is every bit as alive as Satan on planet earth.

At the height of the abolition of slavery movement, Wendell Phillips pointed out the high cost of virtue:

It is easy to be brave when all behind you agree with you; but the difficulty comes when nine hundred ninety-nine of your friends think you are wrong. Then it is the brave soul who stands up, one among a thousand, remembering that one with God make a majority.

You see, I am firmly convinced that you and I can live hopeful lives in the midst of a time in which it is very fashionable to proclaim the imminent end of civilization as we know it. Oh, I would not go as far as J. Peter Vajk has in his popular book, *Doomsday*

Has Been Cancelled.[28] Doomsday may not be called off at all. But whether there is a doomsday or is no doomsday does not affect the story of our lives. There is only one end to our story. Embraced by our loving God, it is a hopeful ending.

23

Hope at the Last: the Best Ending of All

One of the problems in preaching a sermon is the fact you have to prepare it ahead of time. That is, unless you have a huge barrel of past sermons to pull from, which I haven't; or you have so confused your laziness with God's voice that you get up and spout anything that comes to mind at the moment.

My own routine is to research in advance, outline on Tuesday and then spend all day Thursday writing and producing Sunday's "story" of the gospel.

I fully believe that effective preaching is the unfolding of our "story" of God's presence in our lives. Each of us has a "story" to tell and the combination of these stories creates the society's impetus for hope for a meaningful future. But that perspective became problematic for me in the preparation of one particular sermon. You see, as I sat down one Thursday to piece together the story, a church member, Karl Cates, was to have surgery the next day in Mt. Sinai Hospital in New York City. He had a tumor inside his spinal cord. The options were clear. If the fifteen hour surgery was successful, he would, after a year's therapy, return to a normal existence. But if the surgery were to be unsuccessful, he would be paralyzed from the neck down and would perhaps lose his life.

I thought of what the writers for television and movie films would do when faced with such possibilities of good and bad outcomes. They would simply film in advance different endings to cover every possible outcome. Then, if along the way a major actor didn't re-sign his contract, they would already have in the film-can a scene where he died. If the cast did not come off the broken leg of the actress by the wrap-up of the series, they would already have in the film-can an ending with her leg in a cast. And, of course, they would film in advance a happy ending with everyone gathered around a table rejoicing. Then, they would have their endings guaranteed. The ending of the story depends on what happens to the lead characters along the way.

If we were to follow that scenario, then we would write sermon endings to cover good news and bad news. I would simply pull out one ending if the surgery was successful and preach on the power of prayer. If the surgery was unsuccussful, I would pull out another and preach on Job and suffering.

As I sat in Karl Cates' living room and talked with him, both of us marveled at how unlike other stories the story of our Christian life is.

There is only ONE possible ending to the Christian story. It is the same message in success or failure. The events do not change the ending of life for us. It all began that way when Moses went up not to Mt. Sinai Hospital in New York, but to the Mt. Sinai in the desert. There he encountered for the first time the actual presence of God. "Who are you?" asked Moses. The answer returned: "I am who I am." In the Hebrew idiom that means, "I am there wherever it may be . . . I am really there."

What an incredible affirmation of hope that is. "I am there wherever it may be." Regardless of the various twists and turns of individual human stories, God gave Moses the assurance that there would be only one end to the story and wherever that ending was to be found, he would really be there. Consequently, you and I have at the center of the action in our life's story neither an ethical nor a philosophical system, and certainly *not a political reality but fundamentally a relationship with God and a promise that he will ultimately deliver.* What an incredible hope.

Jesus the Christ came to earth and gave us a day-to-day validation of that promise of God in an astounding claim: "I am the resurrection and the life; he who believes in me, though he die, yet shall he live. And whosoever lives and believes in me shall never die." He asked of Martha, "Do you believe this?"

We have heard these words and that story many times before and perhaps the audacity of the statement is lost. Jesus stated as unambiguously as you can get that *there is only one end to the story.* Whether we live to be 13 or 33 or 103, there is only one end to the story. Whether we die tragically or slowly over a long period of time doesn't change the outcome.

Paul correctly told the Galacians that each person must bear his or her own load. The parts we are given to play in the story of life, vary greatly. There are many different chapters in existence. And always we are adding new chapters to the personal history of our lives. So we have to carry our own load No one can live our chapters for us. But Paul is also correct when he claims it is the law of Christ that we bear one another's burdens. If, indeed, there is only ONE end to the story of life, to our personal destiny, and it is the same for all of us, we are ultimately a part of the same ending. If one suffers we all suffer together and if one member is honored, all rejoice together. When the book of your life is shut — the creator writes the same ending in the back for you as he does for everyone else.

What we need to sustain us, then, in the living of our days is *wisdom and cooperation.* The wise person is not necessarily full of information but full of understanding. Regardless of the temporary evidence to the contrary, the wise person knows the certainty of God's judgment, and what is lost may later appear to actually be gain. What is seen on the surface of life is not all there is.

The wise person knows that it is truly possible for all people to be a part of the same story with the same ending in life. Carl Jung, the psychiatrist, noted that a "collective unconscious" works as a part of God's laws. It is the sense of many people being bound up together in a common fate — all suffering with one and all rejoicing with one. It's like the operative force among birds that we observe when we see thousands of birds, with no apparent signals among them, change course and yet leave no one straggling. They possess a communication which tends to make them one. The whole flock can change direction.

I have felt that corporate power. In the birth of our son, Scott, there were difficulties and complications. Emergency surgery was the only hope. I have assisted many people in crisis situations. But I found it a different matter when my own family was involved. To sit there with the doctor in his surgical garb, signing all those papers and deciding on mother or child to live if it came to that, is not easy — not knowing whether in a few hours two people would come back up the elevator or I would just be all alone in life. To put it mildly, all rational approaches to human existence fly out the window in such times. All I could do was wander semi-aimlessly down to the hospital chapel. There, all alone, I felt the flock; not just the prayers of my own local church but the collective spirit of the city. While I was sitting in the chapel, the pastor of the Methodist church walked in. He was my best friend. We sat and talked. We did not verbalize a prayer. The presence itself was a prayer. He told me the intercessory prayer group at the Methodist church was then in prayer for us. My sense of aloneness was transformed into solidarity. I could feel the flock turning with me. Now I'm certain some of the prayers were very sensitive and others were quite immature. But as I sat there I sensed the collective nature of my life. *I was not alone.* Even the horrible prospect of my wife's death and having to start over seemed to be a *reality that would at last be shared.* The whole flock would turn with me if it had to. Somehow I began to understand how sensory clues can affect the will to live. There is only one end to the story, regardless of the time it takes us to get to the end and what we have to go through to get there: the lion will lie down with the lamb, the nations will gather before the throne of God, strangers will be welcomed, and whosoever believes in him will never die.

Do you believe this?

I have observed the collective nature of God's family in the situation with Mr. Cates. A number of people in our local Baptist church were fervent in their prayer life; his wife and I walked into St. Patrick's Cathedral, a Roman Catholic church, and lit a prayer candle. An old Lutheran antique dealer in Pennsylvania prayed for our church and called New York to check on matters for us. The vice president of the United Church of Christ stopped in the middle of his work on the 10th floor at 105 Madison Avenue and prayed hard for us. Then at 10 p.m. one night we sat on his patio in New Jersey and he offered one of the most beautiful prayers on our behalf anyone could imagine. Finally, a number of Jewish people at a place called Mt. Sinai Hospital labored and prayed together for us all. God's flock changed directions without a trace of command.

At the end of a twelve hour stint at the hospital, I caught a bus down toward Grand Central Station. A priest in a collar saw me reading a book on the parables of Jesus. He discerned I must be a minister. I acknowledged that indeed I was. In rapid, staccato fashion he spit out the usual questions: Where do you pastor?

What denomination? How large is your church? In complete sincerity I responded: "Fellow, it really doesn't matter. It just doesn't matter. There's only one end to the story for everybody anyway."

You see, we are all born into a limited earthly family so that we can be given up for adoption into a new family and a new day of birth. Regardless of the tragedies and triumphs, the youthfulness or the age, the circuitous wanderings through valleys of doubt and despair, the painful crawling through suffering and loss, the soaring with praise in the midst of eagles as things turn out all right — we come to only one certain end: "I am the resurrection and the life; he who believes in me, though he die, yet shall he live. And whosoever lives and believes in me shall never die"

We are the trustees of the knowledge of the end of the story of our lives. We owe God an accounting of how we are serving as stewards of that knowledge. If our society cannot expect from us a disciplined character in the face of its uncertainty, from whom can it expect to find it? If it cannot find in us examples of high thinking and plain living so necessary to its own groping in darkness, where are the examples to be found? We are the means whereby the knowledge of the end of life is brought forward from an earlier generation. But we are the means as well whereby generations yet unborn may share a glimpse of their final chapter when you and I have returned to our creator.

The idea is just as scandalous now as it was then — but for all of us, there is still only one end to the story!

It is a hopeful ending — and, because it is, it is the best ending of all. Have hope, my friends, for our world needs it. It is God's gift to us, given to us to share with fellow pilgrims in a technological and scientific world. Indeed, of all God's benefits to us, hope is the rarest gift of all!

Notes

[1] See James B. Dunning, *Values In Conflict* (Washington: National Center of Religious Education — CCD, 1976), p. 51.

[2] This reference has been frequently used by ministers, especially Ewart E. Turner, retired pastor of Grace Church, Lima, Ohio.

[3] Peter Drucker, *People and Performance* (New York: Harper and Row, 1977), p. 142.

[4] Jean-Jacques Rousseau, *The Creed of a Priest of Savoy,* second, enlarged edition, translated by Arthur H. Beattie (New York: Frederick Ungar Publishing Co., 1978), p. X.

[5] See especially the 1979 work by Elaine Heisey Pagels, *The Gnostic Gospels,* winner of the National Book Critics Circle Award and the American Book Award.

[6] Previously published in Harold C. Warlick, Jr., *Conquering Loneliness* (Waco: Word, Inc., 1979), pp. 21-25.

[7] See the characterization of Peter in Frederick Buechner, *Peculiar Treasures* (New York: Harper and Row, 1979), p. 134.

[8] My first exposure to this use of the Roger Bannister achievement came from Dr. Jim Bowers, former pastor of First Baptist Church, Greenwood, South Carolina.

[9] I am indebted to Peter Gomes for the Brice reference. Gomes is Minister and Plummer Professor of Christian Morals, Harvard University.

[10] T. C. Smith was alluded to in a similar manner by C. David Matthews, "Enough Is Enough," *Light* (October 1983), published by the Christian Life Commission of the Southern Baptist Convention.

[11] See Lee Gilbert Highet, *Man's Unconquerable Mind* (New York: Columbia University Press, 1954), p. 17.

[12] See the previously published, "Humankind: Summation of Creation," (Lima, Ohio: C.S.S. Publishing Company, 1980), by Harold C. Warlick, Jr.

[13] C. S. Lewis, *Christian Reflections* (Grand Rapids: Eerdsman, 1967), edited by Walter Hooper, p. X. The quote is from Lewis' sermon, "The Weight of Glory."

[14] Harold Kushner, *When Bad Things Happen to Good People* (New York: Avon Books, 1981), p. 6.

[15] Daniel J. Simundson, *Faith Under Fire* (Minneapolis: Augsburg, 1980), contains a helpful analysis of Job.

[16] A most instructive discourse which heavily influenced my writing on the Isaiah passage is "Strength Not to Faint," pages 43-62 in John Claypool, *Tracks of a Fellow Struggler* (Waco: Word, 1974).

150

[17]*Ibid.*

[18]I am grateful to my friend, John Killinger, pastor of First Presbyterian Church, Lynchburg, Virginia, for the reference to John Mortimer's autobiography. Killinger used the illustration in a sermon by the same title.

[19]As told by Barbara Brokhoff, *Making Angels Sing* (Lima, Ohio: C.S.S., 1982), p. 74.

[20]John Claypool in his sermon, "Authentic Christianity."

[21]Maggie Scarf, *Unfinished Business* (New York: Doubleday, 1980), p. 7.

[22]John White, *The Masks of Melancholy* (Downers Grove, Illinois: Intervarsity Press, 1982), preface.

[23]James Hillman, *Suicide and the Soul* (New York: Harper and Row, 1964), pp. 31-33.

[24]Erwin Stengel, *Suicide and Attempted Suicide* (New York: Jason Aronson, 1974), p. 59.

[25]John White, *op. cit.*, p. 153.

[26]See "Hers," Phyllis Rose, *The New York Times* (April 19, 1984), p. C2.

[27]I am grateful to my friend, Sidney Hall, Chaplain, Hampden-Sydney College, Virginia, for sharing this story with me.

[28]J. Peter Vajk, *Doomsday Has Been Cancelled* (Culver City, California: Peace Press, 1978).

Scripture Index

For those readers who would like to delve into the Scriptures of the Old and New Testaments while reading this book (or for those who are responsible for leading Christian worship, and who may wish to use material in this book in preaching or in sharing with growth groups within a congregation), the following index may prove helpful. We suggest you read each chapter first, then the Scripture assigned to it.

152